D1491036

1 Joseph Rowntree in later years

A QUAKER BUSINESS MAN

A QUAKER
BUSINESS MAN

The Life of Joseph Rowntree
1836–1925

ANNE VERNON

WILLIAM SESSIONS LIMITED
THE EBOR PRESS
YORK, ENGLAND
1982

First published in 1958
by George Allen & Unwin Ltd.

Republished with permission in 1982
by William Sessions Ltd.

©

ISBN 0 900657 63 4

*Text dri-printed from the 1958 edition by Jackson Morley Sessions Ltd.
at The Copy Shop Plus. Plate-printing and binding by
Wm. Sessions Ltd., The Ebor Press, York, England.*

FOREWORD

A great many people helped me in different ways while I was writing this book. I am grateful to those who allowed me access to old letters and family account books, and to those who solved topographical puzzles and checked historical details. Among others too numerous to mention I should particularly like to thank William Wallace, C.B.E., J. Bowes Morrell, Ll.D., Peter Rowntree, B. Philip Rowntree, Joseph R. Naish, John W. Harvey, Roger C. Wilson, B. P. Johnson, M.A., F.S.A., and the staff of the Library of the Society of Friends.

I am much indebted to Jean Rowntree for all her help and suggestions, and especially for reading the manuscript when it was still in an unfinished state.

The following authors have kindly given me permission to quote from their works. Messrs. Urwick and Brech: *The Making of Scientific Management*, published by Sir Isaac Pitman & Son. G. M. Young: *Victorian England, Portrait of an Age*, published by the Oxford University Press. Miss V. M. Clarke: *New Times, New Methods and New Men*, published by George Allen & Unwin. L. E. Waddilove: *One Man's Vision*, published by George Allen & Unwin.

ILLUSTRATIONS

1 *Joseph Rowntree in later years*   *Frontispiece*

2 *Joseph Rowntree and his first wife*   *facing page*   64
   Joseph Rowntree at school in 1848
   Joseph Rowntree in 1868
   Joseph Rowntree at 42

3 *The Rowntree shop in Pavement before rebuilding*   65

4 *The 'Elect' cocoa motor-car*   80
   Taking goods to the station from Tanner's Moat
     factory

5 *View of Haxby Road works (from a drawing)*   81
   Aerial view of Rowntrees' factory in 1956

6 *Factory at Tanner's Moat in the nineties*   128
   'North Street' workshop in the nineties

7 *Joseph Rowntree with Stephen, Seebohm, Arnold,*   129
     and Oscar Rowntree
   Joseph Rowntree and the Very Reverend Dean
     Purey-Cust

8 *Joseph Rowntree at Scarborough, 1912*   144
   Joseph Rowntree at Scarborough, 1920

9 *The Four Generations—Joseph Rowntree, his*   145
   son, grandson, and great-grandson

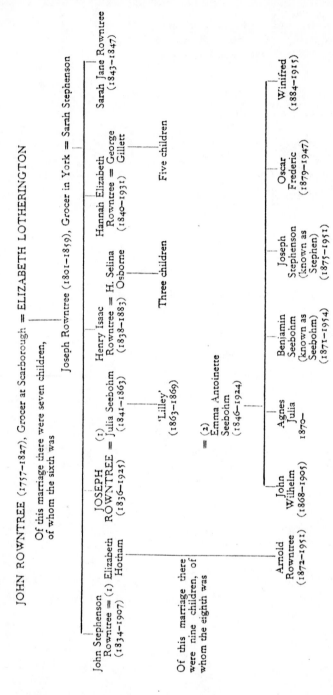

JOHN ROWNTREE (1757–1827), Grocer at Scarborough = ELIZABETH LOTHERINGTON

Of this marriage there were seven children, of whom the sixth was

Joseph Rowntree (1801–1859), Grocer in York = Sarah Stephenson

John Stephenson Rowntree = (1) Elizabeth Hotham (1834–1907)

JOSEPH ROWNTREE (1836–1925) = (1) Julia Seebohm (1841–1863) = (2) Emma Antoinette Seebohm (1846–1924)

Henry Isaac Rowntree = H. Selina Osborne (1838–1883)

Three children

Hannah Elizabeth Rowntree = George Gillett (1840–1931)

Five children

Sarah Jane Rowntree (1843–1847)

Of this marriage there were nine children, of whom the eighth was

'Lilley' (1863–1869)

Arnold Rowntree (1872–1951)

John Wilhelm (1868–1905)

Agnes Julia 1870–

Benjamin Seebohm (known as Seebohm) (1871–1954)

Joseph Stephenson (known as Stephen) (1875–1951)

Oscar Frederic (1879–1947)

Winifred (1884–1915)

This table has been abbreviated, in the interests of clarity, to show only Joseph Rowntree's nearest relations and those who were closely associated with him in business. The marriages of his children have been omitted.

CHAPTER ONE

ON Monday, March 2, 1925, the northern edition of
the *Daily Mirror* carried on its front page a photograph
of crowds of people walking past a newly made grave.
'Funeral of Mr Joseph Rowntree at York' was the caption over
the picture; which was very large and covered practically the
whole sheet. There was just room, in a little box in the top right-
hand corner, for small type to announce, 'New York shaken by an
Earthquake'.

The man whose death in his eighty-ninth year was considered,
temporarily at least, more significant than an earthquake, had
been a citizen of York all his life. Beyond the city, however, his
personality was not very well-known. His name was associated
with cocoa, confectionery, the problem of national intemperance,
the building of a model village, and the establishment of trust
funds to be used for the public good. His career had not been of
the kind which makes news. Yet he had left his mark on a chapter
of history whose true importance is only now becoming apparent, more than thirty years after his death. He had been one of the
people who played a part in the birth of modern industry, and
who saw the development of the pattern from medieval workshop to large-scale factory.

It happened within his lifetime, for his working career lasted
for seventy-one years. He belonged to the generation which stared
at the last stage-coaches in its childhood and the first aeroplanes
in its old age. For him the newspapers had spread headlines about
the Crimean War as well as the Armistice in 1918. There was no
railway to York when he was a little boy, but long before he was
an old man a branch line had been built to serve his own business.
To live through such a span of revolutionary changes is not a
unique experience, but to accept them without prejudice, and to
translate the standards of the past in terms which the future can

9

accept, is an uncommon accomplishment. Joseph managed to do it. And it was done within the uncompromising walls of a factory.

The circumstances were not propitious. The shadows which the Industrial Revolution had cast over men's minds lingered on for years after the 'dark Satanic mills' had been pulled down and forgotten. The belief that machinery was more important than the men who worked it, the employers' unquestioned assumption of absolute authority over their employees, the workmen's loss of interest in their work as factories grew larger and larger—all these things had the seeds of trouble in them.

In his own firm Joseph saw the whole situation developing under his eyes. In 1869 the Rowntree factory was staffed by twelve men, and thirty-five years later there were over three thousand employees in the Firm. In that time all the problems which beset modern industry appeared as fast as the business expanded. How did he deal with them, this man who had served his apprenticeship under the old paternal system?

It is a question worth investigating, since his methods were unquestionably successful. His firm survived its adolescence and emerged as a modern undertaking with no unhappy legacies from an older world and some interesting ideas for a new one.

This was Joseph's contribution to industrial history, and it could, perhaps, only have been made by someone who was not much influenced by the climate of thought which prevailed in his own time. He was not a rebel, but he had some of the qualities of a revolutionary. He did not easily accept the *status quo* in his own business or anywhere else. He was not driven by ambition, and his range of interests did not lie wholly within his factory. Nevertheless, first and last, he was an exceptionally good man of business. Shrewd and serene, intelligent and unassuming, he went his own way without heat or haste, and was not lightly to be diverted from it.

Joseph was born on May 24, 1836, in the last year of William the Fourth's reign. His father owned a grocer's shop in Pavement, in the centre of York, and the family lived above the shop. As she lay in bed after her confinement, Joseph's mother listened to the noise of market-day crowds outside her window, the clamour of geese being walked in from the countryside, and the ring of solid wheels on cobblestones; and in the early hours of the morning she heard the coachman's horn announcing the departure of the 'High-flyer' or the 'Wellington' for London.

The world into which Joseph was born was a place of odd contrasts. The first Act intended to reform Parliament was four years old. It had given the vote to one man in six, but had not done much to disturb the old citadels of the privileged classes. The great land-owners still reigned undisturbed over their villages and acres of farming-land. Here and there hungry farm-labourers burned ricks, but the question of repealing the Corn Laws was not yet taken seriously by many people. The Chartists had not yet drawn up their petition for votes for the working-man; and in mills and factories women and small children worked appallingly long hours in extremely bad conditions.

'England's manufacturing supremacy', Cobbett said, three years before Joseph was born, 'depends upon the toil of thirty thousand little girls.'

It depended, also, on machinery, and this was the age of new inventions. Hardly a year went by without some change in the manufacturing processes of one industry or another. Joseph's mother, as a girl of seventeen, had seen the first railway train in the world running between Stockton and Darlington, and her son was to see the power of steam beginning to be replaced by electricity.

England was called the workshop of the world, but when Joseph was a child about two-thirds of the population still lived and worked in the country. The manufacturing towns were only dark blots on an agricultural landscape, and no one bothered much about what went on in them. 'Outside the orbit of the old ruling class, neglected by their natural leaders, the industrial territories were growing up as best they might, undrained, unpoliced, ungoverned, and unschooled.'[1]

The men of the time often displayed as much inconsistency as did their surroundings. John Bright, fighting the Corn Laws on

[1] C. M. Young. *Victorian England. Portrait of An Age.*

behalf of starving farm-workers, also fought Lord Shaftesbury, who was trying to help the overworked factory-hands. Wilberforce, who did so much to abolish slavery, was also instrumental in keeping his own countrymen helplessly under the thumb of their industrial masters. He was a firm supporter of the Combination Laws, which made the actions of 'associations of workmen' illegal.

The Evangelical movement sent Hannah More distributing pious tracts and bowls of soup among the Mendip Hills, and Wesley's followers into strange districts of northern cotton-towns; but it also made thoughtful men wonder occasionally whether such piecemeal ministrations were all that was necessary. Perhaps it would be better to discover how many people really needed soup? That there would always be families on the edge of starvation was still an accepted fact, but it might be useful to know how many of them there were. The Poor Law Commission of 1832 was the result of some of this questioning, and it was followed by other Parliamentary investigations. The era of statistics had begun.

York, in Joseph's childhood, was not much troubled by the affairs of the world beyond its boundaries. It had no large factories, and the slums within the city walls were a legacy of the Middle Ages, as unquestioned a feature of the place as the Minster itself. The market was the hub of the city's commercial life, and week by week farmers and their wives came in from the surrounding countryside to sell their poultry and vegetables and buy their groceries. The Rowntrees' grocery shop was well placed to catch this country trade, for it stood in Pavement, which was the market-place for 'greens and edibles'.

Joseph's father, who was also called Joseph, had bought this shop in 1822, on his twenty-first birthday. He came to York from his home in Scarborough, riding on the outside of the coach, and probably in a state of some excitement at his own daring. A friend called James Backhouse went with him to the auction, which was to be held at an inn called 'The Elephant and Castle' in Skeldergate. The auctioneer was unfortunately drunk, but at

James Backhouse's suggestion the two young men buried his head in a bucket of cold water and managed to sober him up enough to conduct his business. 28 Pavement became the elder Joseph's property.

The shop and the house had been empty for some time, and the previous owner had gone bankrupt. Everything was rather dilapidated and neglected, but the building itself was a graceful Georgian one, with two bow-windows and a pretty fanlight over the shop door. No doubt it seemed splendid enough to the young man who bought it on the first day of his majority.

The elder Joseph Rowntree was energetic. It took him only a month to put his new house in order and to get his business going, though his 'fittings' were considered unnecessarily elaborate by many of his relations. He had new shop-counters made of mahogany, and a heavy iron shutter was constructed to enclose the passage which led to the house door. In the long drawing-room above the shop there were thick curtains for the three tall windows, and a pierced-steel fender stood in front of the fire-place.

Even at twenty-one the elder Joseph had had ten years' experience of the grocery trade. His father owned a grocer's shop in Scarborough and he had left school at eleven to work in it. For some reason it was not a very flourishing business, and was clearly never going to provide a living both for the elder Joseph and his brother John. So John stayed in Scarborough and Joseph moved to York. An unmarried sister, Elizabeth, went with him to keep house.

It was a very youthful establishment, for his first two apprentices were both thirteen when the elder Joseph engaged them. They lived above the shop with Joseph and Elizabeth, and were regarded as part of the Rowntree family.

Everyone had to work very hard, and the shop was open from six in the morning until eight at night on six days in the week. On market-days it also stayed open until ten-thirty in the evening. There was, of course, no early-closing day; and the only whole holidays, except for Sundays, were Good Friday and Christmas Day. Before the shop opened in the morning Joseph's two boys took it in turn to sweep the place out and fold back the shutters, and at night they had to tidy everything up before they went to bed.

These long hours were universal in the eighteen-twenties, and remained the general rule in most establishments until half-way through the century. And Joseph and his apprentices had, at least, the consolation of success in their work. The first stock-taking showed a balance on the right side, and thereafter the Pavement shop never had a serious set-back in its affairs.

As the years went by the elder Joseph employed more and more young men, and many additions and alterations were made both in the house and in the shop. He had an ingenious mind which took pleasure in working out arrangements for the more convenient running of his business; and he never grudged money spent for the comfort of the household. He discovered, while still young, that it was easier for him to earn what money he needed than to make 'petty economics'.

In 1832 the elder Joseph married Sarah Stephenson, who came from Manchester, and after a week's honeymoon in the Lake District he brought his bride back to Pavement and the responsibilities of a household which now comprised a dozen people.

Sarah Rowntree was only twenty-four at the time of her marriage, but she seems to have been undaunted by the size of her 'family'. She mothered the young apprentices, organized the difficult staggered meals made necessary by the demands of the shop, helped her husband with his accounts, and entertained a great many visitors.

In 1834 the Rowntrees' first child was born, a boy called John Stephenson. Joseph was born two years later, and a third son, Henry Isaac, followed in 1838.

The Rowntrees had been Quakers for several generations, and the beliefs and habits of the Society of Friends coloured their whole way of life. There was a particular flavour about the Pavement household. It was a place where books abounded and where the young apprentices were encouraged to pursue hobbies quite unconnected with the grocery trade. Macaulay's essays were discussed at the dinner table, and the Parliamentary reports were often read aloud. The boys who had spent the morning weighing out sugar or roasting coffee sat down to a midday meal accompanied by the sort of conversation which seldom descended to personalities. 'Servants talk about people; gentlefolk discuss things,' was a Victorian precept. The Rowntrees, by this standard, were gentlefolk.

It was not a word they would have used to describe themselves, for they belonged to an isolated group of people who had no social pretensions. The Society of Friends, in Joseph's childhood, was a body which kept itself deliberately apart from what it often called 'the world'.

George Fox had founded the Society in the middle years of the seventeenth century. Dissatisfied with the existing churches he came at last to the conclusion that set forms of prayer and outward sacraments were harmful, since the symbols of truth too often obscured the truth itself. God dealt directly with every individual soul, and therefore there was no need for 'hireling priests'.

The Quakers were severely persecuted for their beliefs during the first thirty-three years of their existence; and even after the Toleration Act was passed they encountered many lesser inconveniences as they went about their business. Friends who were farmers usually refused to pay tithes, since they would not contribute to support a Church of which they disapproved, and not infrequently their goods and furniture were seized and sold at auction as a result. And they had, also, a number of different 'testimonies' which greatly restricted their choice of a career.

The Peace Testimony, based on the belief that the use of force was unchristian, made it impossible for a young Friend to enter the Army or the Navy. The universities of Oxford and Cambridge were closed to Nonconformists; and although a few Friends were lawyers, not many became artists and none musicians. There was a definite Testimony against swearing an oath, since it implied that there were two sorts of truth, one to be used when a man's hand rested on the Bible and one on ordinary occasions; and there was a strong though unformulated feeling that the arts were dangerous distractions from the true purpose of life.

Very few influences from the larger world entered Friends' families to change or modify their particular character. Until 1859 the penalty for marrying anyone of another religious denomination was to be deprived of membership in the Society, so that generally speaking young Quakers chose Quaker brides. Their children were educated either at home or at Quaker schools. When they grew up, more often than not they went into business. Unless they wished to practise medicine or had exceptional gifts for some branch of science, there was very little else for them to do.

Perhaps there were some who resented the fact that so few careers were open to them, and certainly Joseph's father admitted that his secret ambition had always been to command his own ship. He had grown up beside the sea, and his mother had five brothers, all captains of ships, who had told him wonderful sea stories all his childhood. But his dreams went the way of many others in the history of Friends, and the vision of a ship's quarter-deck was replaced by the counting-house of the Pavement shop.

Yet if there were some frustrated ambitions among the young men of the Society, in these years of its deliberate withdrawal from the world, there were also compensations. The Quakers were generally successful in business. This is not surprising, since the best brains of four thousand families were mostly engaged in trade. The imagination and intelligence which might have made them great actors, fiery advocates, far-seeing generals, or creative artists were devoted to stocking their shelves and satisfying their customers.

Moreover, in the world of business the 'marriage regulations' of the Society had certain advantages. They made for close contacts between family and family, and for a wide knowledge of the financial resources of each one. An industrial aristocracy grew up (though no true Quaker would have countenanced the phrase) which in its way was as closely-knit and well-informed as that of the old landed gentry. A young Cecil might always be assured of a hearing in Parliament because of his ancestry, but a sprig from an established Quaker family had an equivalent advantage when he started in business.

They were business men of a pattern which the twentieth-century has largely forgotten. They pursued, as a side-line, those subjects which circumstances forbade them making into careers. Usually their formal education stopped when they were fourteen or fifteen, but thereafter many of them used their leisure for reading and studying on a scale which would have astonished most schools. The tradition continued until the end of the nineteenth century, when it was still possible to find a steel manufacturer who was a Fellow of the Royal Geographical Society and an authority on British birds; or, in an establishment which displayed the latest feminine modes, a master-draper who was an expert critic of Trollope's novels at a time when they were still unfashionable.

This was young Joseph's background. The disadvantages of it are obvious, the advantages not so quickly apparent. But there *were* advantages; for the Society of Friends, in spite of the drastic limitations it had imposed upon itself, managed to breed men and women of remarkable personality. Some who turned their attention, as did Elizabeth Fry and John Bright, to matters outside the Society, left no uncertain mark on the history of their day. But there were many others whose crisp humour and penetrating judgement survives only in family legends—and in some sound commercial undertakings. They were people whose stature may be measured by the fact that Joseph, a boy who was born and grew up and went to school within the narrow confines of nineteenth-century Quaker society, yet acquired a mental perspective wide enough to be still exceptional half-way through the twentieth century.

CHAPTER TWO

'WE had the reputation of being very wild children,' Joseph wrote in an account of his early years in the Pavement house. 'I think that a stranger, coming into the family, would probably have been startled by the freedom we boys enjoyed.'

Other things might also have startled a stranger, for the relationship between husband and wife, and between parents and children, was an unusual one for the times in which they lived. The average Victorian household of the early forties probably followed a much less rigid pattern than family life was to achieve in the sixties, but even so the elder Joseph was a more familiar and approachable person to his children than most contemporary fathers. Nor did Sarah Rowntree ever pretend to be the gentle, clinging type of woman who was sure that 'Papa knew best' and left all the decisions to him. Neither parent subscribed to the theory that children should be seen and not heard; and somehow, in the crowded quarters above the shop, and in spite of domestic and commercial preoccupations, they managed to make for their family a life which the boys were always to remember as satisfying and exciting.

The Pavement house was not a convenient one. There was no garden attached to it, and on three sides it was hemmed in by a mass of 'little houses and close courts'. When Joseph was born Parliament Street had just been made; a wide thoroughfare which connected the Thursday Market with Pavement. Parliament Street served as the new market-place for the city, and it was an advantage as far as the trade of the shop was concerned; but it also meant that on market-days the Rowntrees' house echoed from dawn to dusk with the noise of crowds.

Even the ingenious plans made by Joseph's father did not quite keep pace with his growing family and his growing trade.

He might lie in bed in the morning thinking out beautiful schemes to make more space for his household, but although he built on a dining-room, and rented both a cellar and an attic from his next-door neighbour, there never seemed to be really enough room. All the apprentices still slept and ate in the house, and there were now twelve of them.

The Rowntrees' private front door opened off a passage leading from the street, and inside it stairs went up to the drawing-room and the kitchen. This kitchen was a horror, even by the standards of the time. It had only one window, giving on to a narrow well above the counting-house, and was infested by rats and mice, which were occasionally found drowned in the filtered water. Mary Tasker, the cook, waged an unceasing fight against the rats, and delighted the little Rowntree boys with tales of her successful kills. There were other drawbacks. One of the elder Joseph's schemes had led to the stocks of sugar for the shop being kept in the kitchen, and even the children noticed the 'dirt and discomfort' caused by a new load being brought in. Last, but perhaps not least, the new dining-room had been built on a different level from the kitchen, and all the meals for twenty people had to be carried up and down half a flight of stairs.

In these crowded years even the handsome drawing-room above the shop did not escape alteration. One end of it was partitioned off to make a bedroom for young Joseph, who was often seen in a white nightgown and cloak making his way to bed through a gathering of his parents' friends.

Such gatherings occurred frequently. The Rowntrees entertained on a vast scale, though their hospitality all centred about the activities of the Society of Friends. No little dinner-parties or musical evenings entered into their social life, but when Quarterly Meetings were held in York seven or eight people would often stay in the house and thirty would sit down to meals in relays. On such occasions Joseph and his brothers slept on mattresses on the floor, so that the visitors could have their beds.

The Society of Friends, though it had cut its members off from many of the usual activities of their contemporaries, had also provided them with numerous opportunies for social intercourse among themselves. The business of the Society was, and still is, conducted through an elaborate system of Preparative, Monthly and Quarterly Meetings, held at different centres all over the country. Sometimes Friends had to travel long distances to attend these gatherings, and to offer them hospitality was counted a duty even if not always a pleasure.

Joseph's mother had her hands as well as her house more than full at the times of Quarterly Meeting in York. Friends had no Testimony against good and abundant food. Indeed, Elizabeth Fry once complained that because so many 'natural tastes' had been forbidden to Friends they took more thought than most about eating, and how food was dressed for the table. Sarah and Mary Tasker must have worked in the dark rat-haunted kitchen for days before every Quarterly Meeting.

Only a woman who was a first-class administrator could have coped with the unwieldy Pavement household. But Joseph's mother was something more than a good organizer. She had a quiet independence of mind which enabled her to pursue a few interests of her own in spite of the claims of children and servants and apprentices.

Quaker women, on the whole, were used to standing on their own feet. They had been trained to it for generations. They were also used to public speaking at a time when, as Doctor Johnson said, female oratory was like a dog walking on its hind legs. It was not surprising that it should be well done, but astonishing that it should be done at all.

In Meetings for Worship, and in their own business meetings —then held separately from those of the men—women Friends had learned to lift up their voices without self-consciousness. And their realistic approach to any problem which confronted them probably startled those who expected to find only meekness under a Quaker bonnet.

In a Society which had abolished 'hireling priests' much pastoral supervision and encouragement had necessarily to be undertaken by ordinary Friends. There were little isolated Meetings scattered up and down the country which had to be visited regularly if they were to be kept in touch with the life of the

Society, there were refractory Friends to be investigated, and those in trouble to be helped and consoled. Women Friends undertook many of these errands, and travelled about their business with a freedom unknown to any other women except the more eccentric members of the aristocracy.

They could not have done it without their husbands' goodwill and support, which indicates an unusual masculine attitude for the early nineteenth century. No man except the most poverty-stricken factory-hand or farm-labourer would normally have encouraged his wife to undertake a task beyond the walls of her own home; and then only acute financial need would have justified such an action.

But the Quaker women went on their journeys with their husbands' blessing; and the men, moreover, were not above keeping an eye on the children during their absence. When Sarah Rowntree went to London she left her year-old son in a nurse-maid's charge, but evidently he spent much time with his father. 'The dear boy is blessed with unbroken health and vigour,' the elder Joseph wrote to his wife, 'but he is pretty good—allows the fire-irons to be undisturbed, though casting upon them a longing eye. His greatest joy is to get into the yard or the shop. The nursery is out of favour. It is too quiet.'

Perhaps, in the long run, the husbands and children of these independent women benefited by the curious freedom they enjoyed. They had something more than gossip to contribute to the pool of their family's interests; and if there could never be for them any preoccupation with balls and gay dresses and the delicate intricacies of social climbing, at least their hobby was not limited by age. To the end of their lives they could trim their souls instead of their bonnets—and other people's, too, from time to time.

They were not, naturally, all saints. There have been female battle-axes in every age, and the elder Joseph refers in a letter to one Hannah Backhouse who 'is gone to Westmoreland Quarterly Meeting, and I know not how she will be borne with there'. On the whole, however, they seem to have been tactful and persuasive in their methods, and there is no doubt that their ministrations saved many an isolated little group of Friends from dissolving altogether.

Sarah Rowntree, for all her competence, left a gentle impression on her children. She was no domestic tyrant, and she had the quality of true humility. If she had to address a meeting of any kind she always prayed that her words might not be found dull and uninteresting. And in all the turmoil of domestic life in Pavement she found time to take drawing-lessons so that she might be a more amusing companion for her children.

There was another side to her nature. She was a woman dedicated to God, and her faith was of the calibre which left no betraying sanctimoniousness behind it in a child's critical mind. Joseph, who attended thousands of Meetings for Worship in his long life, was very seldom moved to break their silence. But once a rather excitable visitor to York Meeting declared that the moment of conversion was known to every soul who had felt the power of the Lord. Joseph rose to his feet. His mother, he said, had had no memory of the hour of *her* conversion, and she was a saint if ever there was one. It is his only remembered utterance in Meeting.

'We had regular school, morning and afternoon, in a little room on the third storey that looked out into Pavement,' Joseph says, in his account of his childhood. 'We had breakfast and dinner in the dining-room, with Father and Mother and the young men from the shop.'

The young men from the shop were important people in the lives of the Rowntree boys. Sometimes they could be persuaded to take the children for walks before breakfast, and once, when a very large kite had been constructed in the nursery, a young man was allowed to leave his work at the counter to help fly it. And there was another apprentice, fond of chemistry and mechanics, who was given leave from his shop time to pursue these studies with John, the eldest Rowntree child.

The apprentices were still, as a rule, boys of thirteen or fourteen when they first arrived to work for Joseph's father. They teased the children of the house, mended their toys, and were

22

occasionally plagued by them. One of the Rowntrees' favourite games, until their mother discovered and stopped it, was to see how far down the stairs they could kick the apprentices' beaver hats without letting them touch the steps.

It was by no means a solemn household, though Bible readings occurred regularly after breakfast, and Joseph and his brothers were required to learn a verse from the Bible every day. Family prayers were becoming an accepted part of the domestic routine in other circles besides the Society of Friends, and responsible men were beginning to see them as part of their duty towards those who lived in their house.

Joseph's father took all his responsibilities seriously. He did not worry about his business, but many other things troubled him constantly. He fretted over the physical and mental welfare of his apprentices. The education committees upon which he served—they governed two Quaker schools, one in York and one at Ackworth—caused him much anxiety of mind. And he was occasionally bothered by the fact that his three young sons were growing up in the cramped rooms over the shop with too little outlet for their energies. He did what he could to remedy this.

'We had joiners' tools given to us,' Joseph remembers, 'and we were encouraged to make collections of plants. *I* made a collection of butterflies and moths, and occasionally on hot summer days our governess would take us to the Langwith Woods where the Comma butterfly and other rare insects were to be found. . . . My brother John tried to make a skeleton of a lark. He hung the dead bird up in the roof, in the hope that time would do the work of the anatomist. But the violation of sanitary laws involved in this experiment led to its premature abandonment.'

In other words Sarah Rowntree tracked down the horrid smell and disposed of the corpse. She was a long-suffering woman, and she needed to be. Dead larks were not the only things she found in the nursery where three high-spirited little boys were leading full and exciting lives. But she had much in common with an American Friend, of whom it was said that she had raised

23

seven children without ever raising her voice, and very few situations could ruffle her composure.

'One of our simple chemical experiments was the manufacture of gas,' Joseph says. 'A little small coal was put in the bowl of a tobacco pipe and covered over with putty. This was placed in the fire, and a small stream of gas soon issued from the mouth-end of the pipe. Another of our favourite occupations was the making of electro-types from plaster-of-Paris casts, and taking gelatine impressions from coins.'

The state of the room after three boys had been let loose with putty, plaster-of-Paris, gelatine, and joiners' tools did not please their governess, but her protests were not very effective.

'Father was always very kind and courteous to our governesses,' Joseph remembers, 'however much he might doubt their management of us. We, as children, knew nothing of such doubts, but supposed that Father and Mother agreed with whatever the governess did.'

They were never much in the governess's power. There was no system in the Pavement house of shutting the children up in the nursery and bringing them down to the drawing-room after tea. They lived, except for their hours of lessons, as part of the big mixed household, with a share in their parents' affairs and a fairly comprehensive knowledge, gleaned from the apprentices, of everything that went on in the shop.

And the elder Joseph, worrier though he might be, was a father to remember. It was not only that he provided the where-withal to make delicious messy experiments. No little boy, lying sleepless in illness or disgrace, ever failed to see his father standing by his bed at some hour of the night.

'There was much comfort in his presence,' Joseph says.

The family lived in the shop-house until Joseph was nine years old. Two more children were born during this time (Hannah in 1840, and Sarah Jane in 1843), and the question of moving into a larger house was frequently debated. The elder Joseph, however, was disinclined to leave Pavement. Like all the family he had a great affection for the house, in spite of its drawbacks. Probably, also, he had an understandable reluctance to join the growing number of prosperous tradesmen who moved away from their businesses to grander establishments in the suburbs. But finally the claims of five children overcame his scruples. In 1845 the family moved to a house in Blossom Street, just outside the city walls.

A married couple were installed in the Pavement household to look after the apprentices, but the elder Joseph still dined with them in the middle of the day, and on Sunday evenings he read aloud to them as he had always done. They were often asked to meals at the house in Blossom Street, and the links between the Rowntree family and their employees were by no means broken. But it was not quite the same as the old family life in the house above the shop; and the responsibility of his 'young men' weighed more heavily than ever upon the elder Joseph.

In Blossom Street the Rowntree children had a garden to play in for the first time in their lives, and their mother was no longer obliged to store sacks of sugar in the kitchen for the shop's convenience. Her domestic circumstances were easier altogether now, and the boys were beginning to go to school as day-boarders.

The Friends' school in York had recently moved from Laurence Street to Bootham when Joseph first became a pupil there. He was eleven years old, a strongly-built boy with the unusual combination of blue eyes and very dark hair. He wore a school-boy's version of the 'plain dress' which was still customary among the Quakers: a dark jacket cut away to show a tightly buttoned waistcoat, and a white shirt with a collar nearly wide enough to cover his shoulders. 'The lads of the city' made fun of this costume, although except for the width of the collar it did not differ very much from their own clothes, and their teasing sometimes came near to bullying as Joseph and his brother John made their way to and from school.

Once inside the school door, however, they were in an atmosphere as familiar to them as that of their own home. The Headmaster was an old friend of their father's, and many of the boys had been known to them all their lives. They settled down comfortably to pursue the same hobbies which they had started in the Pavement nursery.

Joseph's first term was interrupted by an outbreak of whooping-cough, and he and John both caught it. The three other children presently developed it, and Sarah Jane, the youngest, had it very badly. She died on December 19th. Years later Joseph could still remember the stricken look on his father's face on the day when his little sister was buried.

That year the Rowntree family spent Christmas in lodgings at Scarborough. It was hoped that the change of air would benefit the children, and their parents admitted that for once they were thankful to escape 'the bustle of the winter Quarterly Meeting'. It is a confession which reveals their state of mind, for normally they both took a great interest in the business meetings of the Society, and thoroughly enjoyed the gatherings of friends and relations which were part of such occasions.

CHAPTER THREE

JOSEPH spent five years at Bootham School, and the place left its mark upon him. It was rather a curious establishment, very progressive in some ways, and a little old-fashioned in others. The traditional Quaker policy of 'putting a hedge' between the children of the Society and the temptations of the world had weakened by the middle of the century, but at Bootham many of the old customs still lingered. No newspapers were allowed to enter the school, the Headmaster examined all the incoming mail, and no boy was allowed to receive letters except from his own family. There was no form of corporal punishment, but there were 'prolonged sittings in seclusion' which were considered by many to be much worse than a good flogging.

On the other hand, no bounds were set upon intellectual curiosity. There was no subject which the Headmaster, John Ford, was afraid to explore, and no questions which his pupils were forbidden to ask. Only a man whose foundations were built upon rock could have dared to be so adventurous, and his courage was to stand his pupils in good stead later in life, when the world from which their fathers had withdrawn became the world in which they themselves had to live and work. John Ford opened doors for others which he would never pass through himself.

He had, too, some of the splendid inconsistencies of a large-scale character—the stuff of which legends are made. He could be lenient and he could be violent, but he was never dull. He believed that Latin and Greek were essential subjects, and had pronounced views about the best method of teaching them, but he also introduced science into the school curriculum. In the educational world a controversy was raging over the question of teaching science throughout most of John Ford's career, but he does not seem to have been aware of it; and certainly his policy was never questioned by the school's committee. There was no Quaker creed to be challenged by the new scientific discoveries.

The Headmaster was no remote figure to the forty-five or fifty boys who made up the school in Joseph's day. They were his 'family' in the same sense as the Pavement apprentices were the elder Joseph's. Moreover, he believed that a large part of every boy's education went on 'more vigorously *out* of school than it does *in*', and he expected his staff to be the familiar companions of their pupils.

By birth and upbringing John Ford was a member of a closed Society, and he had had no university training and very little contact with other educationalists. But he was, nevertheless, one of the headmasters who looked forward and not backward. In spite of all the minor restrictions he imposed on his pupils they had a progressive education in the widest sense of the word.

Without being aware of it at the time the Headmaster of Bootham was working towards much the same goal as Doctor Arnold of Rugby. They never met or corresponded, but after the Doctor died and his letters and sermons were published, John Ford recognized, with the exhilaration of a traveller on a very lonely road, that in spite of all the differences of creed and caste they had been in agreement about the nature both of God and of schoolboys. Thereafter he often quoted Doctor Arnold to his pupils, and once made a special journey to visit Rugby—a singular tribute from one who had been brought up to distrust all priests.

Under the direction of John Ford's odd and forceful personality young Joseph flourished. He had an enquiring mind, and it was his good fortune to be sent to a school where curiosity was no sin. He joined the Natural History Society, which was the first school organization of its kind in England, and he and his brother John both won prizes for essays on natural history. Of his other scholastic achievements no record remains. Written examinations were introduced during his first year at Bootham, but evidently they were not regarded with the awe and finality of modern times. There is nothing left to tell whether he was near the top or the bottom of his form, but the true value of his schooling may perhaps be measured by his ability to read and enjoy books on very widely varied subjects all his life. He had, also, a scholar's memory, and even in his old age he could usually put his hand on whatever book he wanted in his library and find a particular reference at a moment's notice.

During his schooldays something happened to Joseph which influenced his thinking to the end of his days. He saw the horrors of the Irish potato famine.

It seems a little strange that the elder Joseph should have taken two boys to Ireland at this particular time. Joseph was fourteen, and his brother John sixteen, and although they were told to take their botanical cases and journals with them, and the expedition was represented as a holiday, their father must have known that in a famine-stricken countryside they would be bound to see some of the less agreeable examples of starvation. However he took them, and their Headmaster, John Ford, made the fourth member of the party. It appears probable that the two men had some sort of commission from the Society of Friends to look into conditions in the worst districts with a view to starting relief work.

The memory of that three weeks' journey remained in Joseph's mind until he died. He saw half-dead women sitting by the roadside clutching dead babies. He saw men who lay dying beside a basket of turf which they had carried for miles and failed to sell. He saw places where the dead, uncoffined and unknown, had been laid in trenches by those who were too weak to do more. The schoolboy, with his journal in his pocket and his specimens of plants in his hand, looked and remembered. It was his first encounter with destitution, and it was a landmark in his life.

There was, naturally, poverty in York. There were squalid alleyways and courtyards just around the corner from the Pavement shop where ragged women and barefoot children lived unenviable lives. But Joseph had never seen them dying of hunger. In York there was a 'Soup Kitchen' (which his father had helped to start) and there the poor could get enough nourishment once a day to keep them more or less alive. It was perhaps in Ireland that young Joseph first began to wonder whether soup was really the answer to poverty.

Between 1840 and 1850 no child of an enlightened father could have escaped the knowledge that poverty was the portion of half the population of England. Hood's 'Song of the Shirt' came out in a Christmas number of *Punch*. Cobden and Bright were clamouring for the Repeal of the Corn Laws. Starving farm-labourers were burning ricks. Lord Shaftesbury was producing unbelievable statistics about the conditions of women and children in factories. But hearing is different from seeing. Joseph had never lived in the country, or been inside a farm-worker's cottage. There were no factories in York, and the trail of sleepy, stunted children coming and going to their incredible labours was no part of his experience. It was only in Ireland that he saw, at first hand, exactly what poverty and starvation looked like. He never forgot.

While Joseph was at school the Rowntree family moved again. They went from Blossom Street to a house in Bootham, and Joseph and his younger brother Henry Isaac had now only a very short distance to walk to school. Joseph's surplus energy turned towards athletics, and he won a hundred yards' flat race on the school playing fields. It was a feat of which he boasted a little long after his schooldays were over. But he missed his last summer's cricket because of a broken leg. In an 'excess of high spirits' he jumped a wide ditch on Hob Moor and fell. Legend has it that the leap was twenty-one feet long with an eight-foot descent, and later generations of schoolboys called it 'Joe's Jump'. This was the end of his school career. By the time he could walk again the summer term was over, and he followed his brother John to the Pavement shop.

CHAPTER FOUR

THE heart of the Pavement shop was the counting-house. It was the elder Joseph's private office, and he had made it very cosy. He entertained his friends as well as doing business there, and as long as Joseph could remember there had been comfortable chairs for 'father and his visitors'. A coffee-roasting apparatus was kept in the counting-house, and a tea-kettle could be boiled on it—cups of tea being apparently as much a feature of office life a hundred years ago as they are now. There was also a big double desk, shared by the elder Joseph and John, and above it shelves loaded with old bills and invoices. These shelves, rather curiously, were known as 'David Priest-man's Clothes' because once a bundle of this young man's belongings had been left there for a very long time. 'Look in David Priestman's Clothes' was a familiar cry in the counting-house when an out-of-date address was wanted.

There was a window between the counting-house and the shop, so that the elder Joseph could keep an eye on whatever was going on; and at one time stores were kept in a room whose only door opened beside his desk. But this was not a convenient arrangement, and was presently altered. A good many private conversations went on in the elder Joseph's sanctum which were seriously interrupted by young men coming through for fresh supplies of currants or coffee.

Young Joseph worked as an apprentice for his father. He went home to sleep, but otherwise no difference was made for the son of the proprietor. He obeyed the same rules and did the same jobs as the other young men. The rules had been carefully thought out, and survive in a 'Memorandum' which the elder Joseph wrote in 1852. It was probably sent to people who wished to place their sons with him, and it also served as a guide to 'new boys' coming into the household.

'The object of the Pavement establishment is *business*. The young men who enter it as journeymen or as apprentices are engaged to assist in this business, and are expected to contribute their part in making it successful. The arrangements are such as to afford full opportunity to any painstaking intelligent young man to obtain a good practical acquaintance with the tea and grocery trades, including the purchasing of stocks and the keeping of books. Access is freely allowed to invoices, accounts of sales, cost price of articles, etc.

'It should be understood, however, that the value of the situation in Pavement mainly depends on the temper and disposition of mind of those who enter it. It presents good opportunity for the industrious to learn, but there is little direct business teaching. The place is *not* suitable for the indolent and the wayward.

'In large households punctuality in the time of rising, etc., is important in each member, otherwise the thoughtless or ease-loving individual wastes the time of the others.

'On ordinary occasions only one-half of the Pavement family can take their meals together, hence much time is unavoidably occupied with meals. Without neglecting business much may be done by consideration and arrangement to prevent the needless extension of meal-taking. From the frequency of mealtimes and the general absence of severe labour in the occupations of the family, I think about twenty minutes for each meal is as much as is required. As however it is very desirable that these occasions of meeting together should be of a social and uniting character it is *not* designed to determine their exact duration.

'Every morning, on entering the shop, each young man records in a book kept for the purpose the exact time at which he enters, as shown by the office clock. A gratuity of 26s. per year is allowed to the punctual.

'In the 12th and 1st months [December and January] the shop opens at half-past seven; in the other part of the year at seven. The shop closes at eight, except on market-day nights, when it is kept open until ten.

'The young men are at liberty in the 6th and 7th months to walk [i.e. to be out] until 10 o'clock; in the 4th, 5th, 8th, and 9th months, until nine; and in the remaining six months until a quarter to nine.

'The arrangements of the business allow each young man to attend week-day Meetings every alternate week.

'Opportunity is afforded for every young man to pay a visit to his friends at home during the year. Each young man has a separate lodging room with provision for washing, etc. Smoking and the possession of fire arms are forbidden.

'It is my earnest desire that the household may in all respects maintain those habits and practices in regard to dress, language, etc., which distinguish the religious Society of Friends.'

It is rather a stern prospect, though the shop hours were shorter now than they had been when the elder Joseph started in business, and some boys rebelled against the restrictions imposed upon them. One or two letters written by the elder Joseph indicate that he occasionally had trouble with a 'wayward and indolent' apprentice; but most of them seem to have accepted the conditions of their employment as perfectly natural. They were all Friends, and had probably grown up in families whose pattern of domestic life was much the same as the Rowntrees'. Moreover, they were anxious to get on in the commercial world, and the shop in Pavement was known as an excellent place to learn a trade more difficult then than it is today.

When young Joseph began his career a grocer needed a good deal of skill and discernment if his business was to succeed. Tea and coffee both had to be blended, and as well as the standard China and Indian teas which were made up for general sale some particular customers demanded a special mixture of their own. It took a fine palate to achieve the same result time after time, for even the best teas, such as Oolong, were apt to vary with every consignment.

The same thing was true of most of the goods arranged on shelves and in drawers against the handsome mahogany panelling which lined the Rowntree shop walls. There were usually five or six different grades of butter on sale, and even cheeses bought at the same time from the same dairy often varied and had to be priced accordingly. The flour which came from local mills was seldom identical in quality every year, and the great hogs-heads of Demerara and Barbados sugar all had to be tested before their contents were sold.

To assess the merits of all his different stocks was the grocer's business. There were very few proprietary articles whose standard could be guaranteed wherever they were bought, and housewives depended almost entirely on the judgement of their local shop-keeper. His goods carried his own name as a guarantee of satisfaction, and his reputation, in the strictest sense, was a personal one. Young Joseph, who later became almost fanatical about the quality of his own wares, learned his standards in the days when he worked between the polished counters and the warehouse of the Pavement shop.

We know a little about the boys with whom Joseph worked when he first left school. Three years before he started to earn his living in Pavement—in 'third month of the year 1849'—the York Bond of Brothers was established. It is an imposing title, but it was in fact simply a small club formed 'to keep alive the friendship and interest which existed among the members during their tarriance with Joseph Rowntree at York'.

The Bond resolved:

'(1) To meet on the steps of York Minster at 12 noon of the thirtieth day of sixth month 1860.
'(2) Each member to write annually, before the thirtieth of sixth month, and give the President an account of his proceedings during that year.
'(3) The President to write a report of the proceedings of the whole Bond and forward it to each member.'

These 'proceedings' are such as might be expected from young men setting out in the world to make a living. George Pumphrey, who was the eldest apprentice in 1850, and his brother Thomas, the youngest apprentice in the same year, both went to Newcastle in 1854, and there took over an old-established family grocery. 'Cholera is carrying off its hundreds,' Thomas writes to the

Bond, 'and the young man who had previously managed this shop has commenced within a few doors of us and is carrying off many old customers. But hope on, hope ever!'

William Hughes occupied 'Number One Position, Tea side', in the Pavement business in 1850. In 1851 he was foreman and the next year he lived in the business-house and shared the responsibility of looking after the other apprentices with Rachel Rowntree, a relative of the elder Joseph's. In 1854 William was the 'last of our club in the old city' and expected to report a change of position next year.

Some of the young men went south and west to Bath and Bristol and Devizes. They tell of their successes and their difficulties, of putting plate-glass windows in their shops to attract customers, of employing 'one *very* small boy, and an extra one on market days', of engaging a housekeeper who is to be *only temporary*, heavily underlined.

Most of them married and recommended the rest to do likewise, and nearly all express a firm determination to keep the appointment on the Minster steps in June 1860. The elder Joseph, on hearing of the Bond, asked them all to dine with him on that day; but he was dead before the Bond's date for meeting came round. And as the record of their proceedings ends in 1859 we do not know how many gathered at twelve noon on the Minster steps.

The York Bond of Brothers dissolved after 1860, as was natural and inevitable now that its members were scattered and grown-up, but its existence bears witness to the success of the elder Joseph's ambition to make his apprentices feel part of a community as well as a business. Their free time may have been much restricted by present-day standards, but obviously they were not lonely. They were still a 'family'.

Young Joseph once described himself as a 'very raw youth' when he first left school, and he had a natural diffidence which often kept him silent among his elders. But his father had a natural gift for conversation, and the Pavement dinner table was one which 'even a boy found interesting', Joseph says. He adds that 'the young men present would sometimes be little accustomed to maintain a conversation, but my father always succeeded in drawing forth whatever stores they possessed'.

The elder Joseph was, furthermore, the sort of man in whom people confided. He was intuitive and sympathetic, though he had a most penetrating eye for the weak point in an argument. This, it is said, was 'sometimes found discouraging by those who applied to him for counsel'. It was obviously no use asking the elder Joseph's advice if you had something to cover up, or were trying to rearrange facts for your own convenience. There were many people, nevertheless, who came to his counting-house for help in a private difficulty as well as to discuss public affairs. He was elected an alderman of the city the year after Joseph left school, and then the number of callers at the Pavement shop increased still further. There was talk in the counting-house about draining the evil-smelling Foss river, which ran close behind the Rowntree warehouse; and there were discussions about the use of 'steam-engines' in the city, and the nuisance caused by their smoke. And always, naturally, there were Friends who came to talk about matters concerning the Society.

It was in these years that the elder Joseph was trying to get the Quaker Marriage Regulations altered. For generations the Society of Friends had disowned those of its members who married anyone of another religious denomination. There were two objections to such marriages in the minds of Friends. One was simply to 'marrying out', since to be 'unequally yoked' was obviously a situation full of potential difficulty. The other objection, and the stronger of the two, was the fundamental Quaker disapproval of any union celebrated by a priest. But as a Friend could not, by law, marry a non-Friend in Meeting, 'marrying out' generally meant marriage by a clergyman; and this incurred the full weight of the Society's condemnation.

Sometimes people were reinstated as members of the Society even after they had married against the rules; but, nevertheless, the practice of disownment was a suicidal one for the Society as a whole. Nearly five thousand Friends were deprived of membership in the first half of the nineteenth century, and in spite of this the elder Joseph encountered much strong conservative obstinacy among his fellow Quakers when he began to urge the necessity for altering the regulations.

There were some, however, who supported him, and among them was John Bright. Bright had seen a dearly loved sister cut off from the Society when she married, and when he heard that the elder Joseph was trying to get the rules changed he gave him all the support in his power, both in public and in private. His appearances at the shop were always exciting to the young men behind the counter, who looked with awe on the man who had made history by getting the Corn Laws repealed.

John Bright was one of young Joseph's heroes. There was twenty-five years between them in age, but they had many ideas in common. John Bright was much concerned with the state of Ireland, and in his Parliamentary speeches and his articles Joseph found descriptions of the horrors he himself had seen. There was, too, a dramatic quality about John Bright which many Friends distrusted, but which appealed strongly to the young. If his presence at Quaker gatherings was not always a source of 'unmingled gratification' to the Elders, it was usually exciting to the younger members of the Society. 'His conversation and his bearing give the impression of great power,' was the verdict of Joseph at nineteen.

Three years went by uneventfully while Joseph was learning his trade, learning to talk to his father's callers, and devouring the books in his father's library. The family had now moved for the last time. They were established in a large house on the corner of Bootham and St. Mary's, which the elder Joseph had built for his retirement. It was not a beautiful house, but it was spacious. There was plenty of room for a boy to shut himself up and read, and Joseph read enormously. He read history, philosophy, the novels of Jane Austen, and two books which shook the English world of their day: Darwin's *Origin of Species* and John Stuart Mill's *Liberty*. He was laying his foundations.

CHAPTER FIVE

JOSEPH'S grandfather had ridden on horseback from Scarborough to London at the end of the eighteenth century in order to attend the Yearly Meeting of the Society of Friends, which is a representative gathering of the whole Society. His father, in the twenties and thirties, had travelled from York to London by the High Flyer coach on similar occasions. Joseph, in 1855, went by train. He was accompanied by his father and his elder brother, he was just nineteen, and he was as nearly excited as it was possible for one of his temperament and training to be. He and his brothers had been encouraged by their father to keep a journal on all their excursions from the time they were very small boys. For this journey to London Joseph had provided himself with a strongly bound little notebook containing beautifully thick blue ruled paper.

The journey itself was not uneventful.

'When we stopped at Grantham,' young Joseph records, 'a lady . . . asked Father rather earnestly for *The Times*. She glanced hastily over the columns of deaths, then sunk back into the corner of the carriage and burst into an uncontrollable fit of weeping. When she was a little composed she pointed to the notice of the death of her brother, killed in the trenches before Sebastopol.'

The Rowntrees had come to attend Yearly Meeting, and they missed none of the sessions. But they had two clear days before the first session, and in these two days Joseph went sight-seeing. He went to Madame Tussaud's ('the figures, though life-like, were not so deceptively so as I had been led to expect'), and he went to see the Thames Tunnel and the Zoo. The animals appeared to him healthy and comfortable, and he particularly admired the fish.

Even when Yearly Meeting was in full swing there was time

for some social distraction. The Rowntrees and the Pumphreys visited Ham House, in a carriage kindly sent by Samuel Gurney, and one Sunday afternoon they went to tea with Joseph J. Lister. There young Joseph again met John Bright, who was extremely unpopular at this time because of his opposition to the Crimean War. Nevertheless, Joseph heard him say that 'amidst great opposition he had some encouragement. About thirty ministers who were personally unknown to himself had written to him expressing their approval of his conduct'.

Although the Crimean War was not discussed at length in the Yearly Meeting sessions at Devonshire House in 1855, John Bright made his presence felt among Friends almost as strongly as among members of Parliament.

Joseph notes that Bright had a 'great objection to so much power centralizing in the body of Friends in London', and during another session he had a good deal to say on the subject of Friends acquiring a special piece of unconsecrated ground for their dead. Joseph reports Bright's speech.

'It was a considerable expense to buy a piece of land and wall it round for a Meeting the size of that to which he belonged. There were not more than three interments a year. The place, when bought and walled, looked more like a cattle-pound than a resting place for the dead. But that which weighed on his mind more than any other consideration was that in a society like ours separated by so many sectarian differences from the world, it was well to merge these differences in death. It was well after the conflicts and struggles of life to meet in one common resting-place.'

These sentiments cannot have been generally popular. Joseph records them without comment, but it is clear where his sympathies lay. Towards the end of Yearly Meeting he notes that John Allen '*hoped* that Friends would advocate peace principles in a peaceable manner, whether in the *house of commons* or anywhere else'. The italics are Joseph's and so is the lack of capital letters. He knew his hero by now; and peaceful methods, as the term was generally understood by Friends, were no part of John Bright's make-up. He pleaded for peace with a forcefulness which the Society distrusted.

39

Joseph went back to York with his mind full of the sights and sounds of London. The City had taken hold of his imagination and he wished to know it more intimately. There is no record of the means by which he persuaded his father to let him live and work in London, but the arguments of young men thirsting to see something of the world beyond their home town do not differ very much from one century to another. No doubt Joseph pointed out—quite truthfully—that now his apprenticeship was nearly over both he and the shop in Pavement would benefit if he had some first-hand experience of another grocery business before his father took him into partnership. It was not an uncommon practice for young men to polish off their knowledge of trade in such a way. George Cadbury, who was later to build up the great Bournville factory, worked as an assistant in the Rowntree shop for two years while Joseph was still an apprentice there.

Joseph got his way, and in February 1857 he was established in lodgings in London and working at a big wholesale grocer's in the City. He wrote to his father:

'I generally arrive at Fenchurch Street about 8.30. During the morning brokers are frequently bringing in samples of tea, which I liquor against those we have in stock. In the same way I roast, grind, liquor and taste the samples of coffee. The roasting, to do it perfectly, is a very delicate operation, and I am glad to take every opportunity of increasing my skill.

'I frequently accompany one of the clerks to the Customs and the Docks and also to the Banks. I am gradually getting to understand the system of book-keeping.

'I also intend to look over the places of business we deal with, where there is likely to be anything new to learn; and I mean to see some sugar-refining, and to visit a first-rate grocer in the West End.'

The elder Joseph may have smiled over that letter. He was considered an authority on coffee himself, and in 1853 he had been consulted by Gladstone, who was Chancellor of the Exchequer at the time, on a technical point concerning the sale of coffee mixed with chicory. But he was a tolerant man. He realized that young Joseph was at the age when every right-thinking youth considers his elders hide-bound old fogies. He would find out, in time, that the Pavement shop knew very well the needs of its market-day customers from the country, and had little that was useful to learn from a grocer in the West End of London.

When the day's work was over, and the big wood-heated coffee-roaster which needed so much anxious tending had been cleaned and left to cool, young Joseph went off to the gallery of the House of Commons.

It was the early days of the rivalry between Gladstone and Disraeli, and to a young man interested in politics the debates often provided as much drama as an exciting film does for the adolescent of today.

Joseph was not impressed by Disraeli. 'His utterance is hesitating—his argument not very clear—his brilliance seems only to display itself in satire—his arguments seem saturated with party feeling.'

This criticism occurs in an account of the Budget debate of February 21, 1857, and it was possibly Joseph's first visit to the House, for he had been only three days in London.

'Disraeli's successor', he goes on, 'was the poor Chancellor of the Exchequer, who delivered an answer that would have wearied an audience less fastidious than the Commons. He held in his hand a bundle of papers similar to those we keep in a drawer in the shop marked "paid bills". These he continually turned over, apparently looking for the right one, and his difficulty in speaking seemed little less than his difficulty in finding the paper he sought.'

The young grocer was something of a connoisseur where speech-making was concerned. For years he had been reading, and listening to his father read, the Parliamentary reports. Moreover, he had been brought up in the Society of Friends, an audience with a fine critical appreciation for the matter of any public utterance, though they might be tolerant of the manner in which it was delivered.

In this debate only Gladstone came up to Joseph's standard. 'It was, I think, the finest oratorical display I ever heard,' he says. 'The tendency to refine, which was said to diminish the force of his earlier speeches, seems to be now rubbed off. But that which gives the most force to his speeches, and contrasts strongly with Disraeli, is his evident sincerity and earnestness. What struck me on this occasion . . . was his very sparing use of satire.'

The House of Commons continued to be exciting. A week after the Budget debate there was trouble in China. Canton was bombarded by order of an over-zealous British Minister in Hong-Kong, who had unfortunately not verified his facts before giving the command to fire. It seems indisputable that the Minister was in the wrong; but the Government were apparently not prepared to reprimand him until Cobden, in Parliament, brought forward a motion condemning the attack.

Cobden had not been much in the public eye since the Repeal of the Corn Laws ten years before, but on this occasion he impressed the House.

'It was very interesting', Joseph wrote to his mother, 'to listen to the carefully stated and clearly arranged facts, to the unanswerable arguments and earnest appeals of Mr Cobden. . . . Without any pretension to oratorical power his speech was impressive and was listened to with respect by the House. Indeed, his case was so strong that ministers knew not how to answer it and had to resort to those appeals which always find some approvers, about the "Honour of the British Flag", etc.'

It was an American, Oliver Wendell Holmes, who said, 'We are all vehicles in which our ancestors ride'. In young Joseph they rode very strongly. He was, in the quaint boast of an older Friend, the 'fourth generation of the unbaptized'. For over a hundred years his forbears on both sides of the family had declined to be taken in by high-sounding phrases. The reference to the British Flag was something he distrusted, and his conception of honour was far removed from an easy patriotic formula.

On this occasion in Parliament Joseph's private judgement was endorsed by the House itself. Men from both sides supported

42

Cobden, the Government were placed in a minority of sixteen, and an appeal to the country followed.

Joseph naturally took a great interest in the general election. He describes the scenes at the nominations in the Guildhall and mentions the daughters of Baron Rothschild, who came in a carriage, accompanied by a page, to visit some of the City of London electors. The result of the election was, however, a disappointment. Cobden, Bright, Layard, and many other leading opponents of the Chinese policy lost their seats.

'Lord Palmerston has been successful in excluding most of the troublesome M.P.s from the House,' Joseph writes home sadly.

In York the elder Joseph was not altogether happy about his son's preoccupation with politics.

'I do not wonder at thy feeling interested in the debates,' he writes. 'I should do so if I were in thy position. But I would not have thee to allow thy mind to be *deeply* engaged with them, or to attend the House very frequently.'

Friends were still far from convinced that it was wise for them to enter 'public life'. John Bright, standing as candidate for Durham in 1843, had met with much disapproval among his friends and relations. 'I don't like my son pushing himself to the front,' his father had said.

The elder Joseph Rowntree, fourteen years later, may have had an uneasy feeling that his son, too, might wish to stand for Parliament. If young Joseph *had* chosen a political career his father would probably have supported him. He was a very understanding man, and he knew something of the frustration caused by stifling young ambitions; for his own regret that he had not been able to go to sea never quite disappeared. But he definitely hoped to see his son in the Pavement shop, and not in the House of Commons.

Young Joseph did not defend his interest in politics. He continued to visit the House of Commons—though perhaps not quite as constantly as before, since he had a real respect for his father's wishes—and he tactfully ceased writing home long accounts of the debates. Instead he filled his letters with more Quakerly matters: a visit to the Friends' School at Sibford near

Banbury, dinner with the aged Peter Bedford, known as the 'Spitalfields Philanthropist' from his work among the silk-weavers of that densely populated district, and a week-end journey to Hitchin to stay with family friends.

There was a particular reason for his visit to Hitchin, though Joseph does not mention it in his letters home. A girl called Julia Seebohm, whom he had known while she was a pupil at the Friends' school in York, was staying with her relations at Hitchin that spring.

Julia's father, Benjamin Seebohm, was German by birth, but he had been connected with English Friends since his boyhood. His parents, who belonged to a group of German Quakers in Bad Pyrmont, traced their association with Friends from the visit of an Englishwoman—daughter of William Tuke of York —about the year 1800. The Bad Pyrmont Meeting was again visited by four English Friends in 1814, and one of them was Sarah Hustler of Bradford. Young Benjamin Seebohm was asked to act as interpreter for these visitors. He proved so useful that he was persuaded to go with the English party not only to Minden and Frankfort but also finally to Switzerland and the South of France. By this time Sarah Hustler had taken a great fancy to the young German. On the way from the South of France to Calais she suddenly said that she would like him to return with her to England, and that she had his father's consent for him to do so. Benjamin, though surprised, agreed to visit Bradford. He was not quite seventeen, and Sarah seems to have been a masterful woman.

As soon as they were settled in her house at Undercliffe, near Bradford, Sarah proceeded to arrange her young protégé's life for him. She directed his English studies, particularly his reading of the journals of early Friends and the history of the Society. She took him about with her on visits to relations, and to Monthly and Quarterly Meetings. Finally she arranged for him to be apprenticed to a woollen-cloth manufacturer near Huddersfield, at the same time as her nephew John. She found lodgings for the two boys in the same house, and when they had finished their apprenticeship they set up in business together in Bradford.

44

Sarah Hustler had recognized in young Benjamin qualities which were to be of value to the Society of Friends, for he became a notable figure in the religious world of his day; but he was never successful in business. His long and frequent 'journeys in the ministry' kept him away from home for months, and sometimes for a year at a time. Such absences are not usually conducive to the prosperity of a business, and his wife was left on one occasion with absolutely no income at all.

Benjamin had married Esther Wheeler, of Hitchin, in the year 1831. She was a granddaughter of William Tuke of York, and all her forbears on both sides were of old Quaker stock. She had need, in her married life, of all her inheritance of courage and endurance; but by the time Joseph Rowntree met Julia, the youngest child of the family, Esther's life had become less harassed. Benjamin had retired early from business (perhaps because of 'difficulties' which are mentioned in some contemporary letters but are never explained) and made a modest living by editing the *Annual Monitor* and the *Lives* of various 'Weighty Friends'.

The Rowntrees and the Seebohms had been friends for many years. Before Joseph himself was born his grandmother had noted in her journal that 'Benjamin and Esther Seebohm were at Whitby Meeting, and appeared in testimony very acceptably'. The Seebohm boys had been educated at Bootham School, and the younger one was Joseph's contemporary there. Julia, the only girl in the family, was at the Quaker school in Castlegate for three years. She left just before it was moved to new buildings and changed its name to The Mount. Young Joseph had noticed her sitting in York Meeting, wearing a plain drab-coloured dress and a poke bonnet of grey beaver or Tuscan straw, according to the season. The straw bonnets had white ribbons and a little 'curtain' to cover the back of the neck, and these curtains were sometimes made of 'regrettably frivolous material' and earned the reproof of the school authorities.

Julia was not strong, and her mother knew all the sanitary drawbacks of the Castlegate school, for she had once acted temporarily as its headmistress. She asked Sarah Rowntree to keep an eye on her daughter's health, and Julia was a frequent visitor to the Rowntree's house while she was a schoolgirl. But in this spring of 1857 she had left school, and Joseph went to meet her at a safe distance from that parental supervision which is inevitably a trial to the young, no matter how benevolent it may be. And here at Hitchin were laid the foundations of a love affair which in due course ended in marriage.

There is no doubt at all that Joseph admired as well as loved both his parents. But the freedom and anonymity of a great city were a delight to him after his upbringing and schooling in a provincial town among a little group of people who existed in a world of their own. Evidently in his letters home he said nothing about the date of his return, for on April 17th his father wrote, 'Thou wilt be surprised to find that John purposes being in London on second-day evening. We thought that in the existing conditions of our sugar stocks it would be worth while for him to come . . . I should like to know thy own views as to returning, whether at the close of Yearly Meeting, or of extending thy stay.

'Our stock-taking, as thou wilt recollect, falls in course in the first week of fifth month. At this time I look to thy receiving a share in the business . . . Possibly John may converse with thee upon it; and if he should I would encourage thee frankly to mention anything which has occurred to thee as claiming notice.'

The elder Joseph wanted his son at home. He was evidently not very happy about him in London. But the pressure brought to bear on young Joseph, who was about to celebrate his twenty-first birthday, was so light that it could hardly be called pressure at all. Perhaps his father still remembered his own feelings at the same age, when he had bought the Pavement shop and established his independence. Perhaps he still thought occasionally of his father's and brother's warnings and his mother's worried questions. They had been unnecessary and a little annoying. So he wrote very guardedly to his son, hinting only that as a partner his presence in Pavement would be desirable, and promising that his suggestions about the management of the shop would be listened to with attention. But one wonders if the state of the sugar stocks *really* necessitated John's journey to London at this particular moment, or whether the older brother was sent to see whether young Joseph did really mean to come home or not.

Joseph said at once that he was coming back to York at the end of May. No doubt he would have liked a few more months in London, but, in a phrase often used by his grandmother, they would have been an 'improper indulgence'. He bought another solid little notebook and prepared to meet his father and attend the Yearly Meeting sessions with him.

This Yearly Meeting of 1857 was an important one for the elder Joseph. He had to introduce a minute from Yorkshire Quarterly Meeting on the Marriage Regulations of the Society —the subject which had taken up a great deal of his time and energy for the past three years.

'He brought the minute forward,' young Joseph says, 'not at great length, but sufficiently so, I should have thought, to convince every truth-seeker.'

Yearly Meeting, however, was *not* convinced. The question was debated until nine o'clock in the evening, but all that was attained was a minute 'recommending the subject to the favourable consideration of next year's Yearly Meeting'.

Perhaps things would have gone differently if John Bright had been present; but he was in Italy with his daughter, recovering from a long and severe illness.

Another question which was raised in this year, and also postponed, 'to the astonishment of not a few', was that of 'plain dress'. It was still, at this time, required of Friends to bring up their children, servants, and those under their care, in 'plainness of speech, behaviour, and apparel'. One member of Yearly Meeting spoke at some length on this subject. He did not think the youth of his Quarterly Meeting were unmindful of the duty of plainness, but many of them 'did object to hear about a mark unsanctioned by Christianity'.

Another Friend objected, says Joseph, 'to the *pointed* allusions to the frailties of the dead. He thought a certain lady's ministerial defects were no greater than those of many others'.

All in all, it does not seem to have been one of the more satisfactory annual gatherings of the Society, and a rather depressed family party travelled back to York when it was over. Young Joseph was sorry to leave London, and his father was suffering from the reaction which follows a long effort. But the Marriage Regulations over which he had worked so hard were still unchanged.

CHAPTER SIX

A
T twenty-one Joseph was an energetic young man, quick
and decisive in all his movements. Out-of-doors he had
a habit of walking very fast, with his head tilted back at
an odd angle which made him appear to be looking at something
in the sky. Dark hair framed a face whose natural expression, in
the language of the time, was 'pensive and serious'. But in the
Pavement shop both the apprentices and the customers found him
alert and cheerful. He particularly liked market-days, when the
place was crowded with country people.

'On these days', one of his young apprentices said, 'he was all
activity, and his voice rang out over all the others as he called out
his orders.'

The same apprentice remembered gratefully that Joseph had
several times got him out of a muddle. He came up once to
Joseph and the foreman in the shop with what he describes as a
'silly question' about the making up of a customer's book. The
foreman gave him an explanation which he did not understand in
the least. Joseph saw his confusion and said, 'Let me show this
young man how to do it in the very *brightest* style'. He took up
pen and paper and explained the mystery, giving reasons and
examples. It was a piece of tactful diplomacy. The young man
had no further trouble with customers' books; neither had the
foreman's authority been undermined or the apprentice's stupid-
ity exposed.

But the same apprentice, later on, was firmly reproved by
Joseph for nicknaming and making fun of certain venerable
Friends who spoke at Meeting.

'They have come from a distance,' Joseph said, 'and given up
time to serve our interests. We should not belittle their efforts.'

There was still no nonsense tolerated from 'wayward' apprentices in the Pavement shop; though it is unlikely that the young-

est partner in the firm was often obliged to brandish his authority. He got on easily with young men, and about six months after his return from London he began to teach in the Adult School which met every Sunday morning in a room that had once been a wood-turner's shop just behind the Rowntrees' warehouse.

This Adult School was the offshoot of a 'First-Day School' started by York Friends in 1848. The original Sunday morning classes had been intended for boys between eight and fifteen, but almost at once a few adults joined them. The men came because the classes provided a chance of learning to read and write; and this meant that they were serious-minded people who were prepared to work hard. There were thirty of them by 1857, and at this point it clearly became desirable to separate them from the more frivolous younger fry. So a room behind the Rowntrees' premises in Lady Peckitt's Yard was rented, and the men's class moved there from the British School in Hope Street, where all the classes had previously been held.

In Lady Peckitt's Yard the men's class was divided into two. Joseph took 'B' class and his older brother John took 'A'. John had a firm hold on his pupils' affections. He had begun his first lesson by distributing a plum cake among them and announcing that they would read the Bible straight through. He then embarked upon the first chapter of Genesis. This was the kind of good solid food, spiritual and material, which his hard-working scholars could appreciate. From Joseph they were to get something a little more speculative.

Joseph was twenty-one when he first took charge of a class of nine men, most of them older than himself. He was nearly sixty before he stopped teaching in the Adult School every Sunday morning. In those forty years many things changed. By the end of them it was no longer necessary to teach grown-up men to read and write, and Social Clubs and Libraries, Allotments and Saving Funds, had all become associated with Adult School work. But the Scripture lesson remained as important as it had been in the beginning, and every week Joseph produced a carefully-thought-out thesis to catch his pupils' attention.

Even at twenty-one he was no brash young man. He once

wrote to a friend: 'You cannot enter upon this work with less qualification than *I* had when I began. To prepare a bright and practical address once a week may be of immense educational value to oneself, but it is an onerous task. . . . However, it becomes a little easier with practice.'

The numbers in Joseph's class rose slowly but steadily. Not only was he patient with men who laboured over unfamiliar pot-hooks, and took a very long time to graduate from 'large-hand' to 'round-hand' and finally to 'small-hand', but he was also interested in his scholars as people. From them he learned to translate his political theories into facts. He followed up his Sunday classes with week-day visits; and in the houses of his pupils he began to see quite clearly what poverty meant to the respectable poor. It shed a useful light on a subject which was never far from his thoughts.

The fact that John and Joseph, sons of a prosperous master-grocer, were able to get on terms with their Adult School pupils speaks well for the two young men. They were dealing now not with members of their own religious society, but with men of different denominations, for the school was open to all. There must have been a real classlessness and much true humility in both the young Rowntrees, or they could not have won trust and even affection from men so much older and less fortunately placed than themselves. Had there been any kind of priggishness in their teaching their classes would soon have melted away. But the Adult School never melted away. It had its ups and downs, but it lived to celebrate its fiftieth birthday, and to serve as the forerunner of much other social work.

In May of 1858 Joseph went for the third time to Yearly Meeting in London. In this year a different note is heard among the speeches at several of the sessions. 'It was *not* a time of unbroken sunshine,' the elder Joseph writes to his eldest son. Nevertheless things were moving. John Bright was back again, and although still convalescent he was quite well enough to address Yearly Meeting on the Marriage Regulations of the Society. The Meeting was not anxious to hear him. Several times

51

he stood up, failed to catch the Clerk's eye, and had to sit down again. But John Bright was not easily defeated. His speech, when it came, was a denunciation of the blistering sort to which he had accustomed the House of Commons.

'Hundreds of our members—aye thousands—have been disowned for acts for which no church could rightly disown. It was opposed to Christianity, it was opposed to philosophy, it was opposed to all sound argument *and* to common-sense to disown for these marriages. . . . There was no use attempting to put people in strait-jackets. That was the fault which had been committed by other churches and which we are all now struggling against.'

So young Joseph reports the man he admired. But the Society of Friends was less susceptible to rhetoric than most of John Bright's audiences. They heard him out—and adjourned the Meeting.

Later, however, it was agreed to refer the whole matter to a committee which was to report its findings in a year's time.

It was a disappointing conclusion, but nevertheless young Joseph believed that the matter was nearly settled; and as it turned out he was right. Next year, at the last Yearly Meeting of the elder Joseph's life, the 'proposition from Yorkshire Quarterly Meeting' was adopted, and the Marriage Regulations were altered.

There is a voice which speaks in an aside in the history of Friends. Those who have known the older generation of living Quakers will recognize it. It has a note of dry wit, a genius for under-statement, and a practical shrewdness. It is possible to hear an echo of it in the words of old Jacob Bright, John Bright's father, who once met upon the highroad a man whose horse had broken its leg and would have to be shot. Friends and neighbours were condoling loudly with the unfortunate owner, but Jacob turned briskly to the man standing next to him. 'I'm sorry five pounds—how sorry art thou?' he enquired, and then took up a collection in his hat.

The same practical line was taken by one of a pair of Friends who went to investigate the case of a girl who intended to 'marry out'. As they left the weeping young woman (she had refused to reconsider her decision) one of the visitors suddenly turned back. 'Don't cry, lass,' he said, 'if thee wants the man *have* him.'

There are plenty of letters and memoirs telling of the spiritual graces and virtues of ancient Friends, but not many which record this caustic though always unmalicious humour. Only, by chance, a memorable under-statement sometimes slips through the pious histories to remind their descendants that these worthy men were not always solemn, and that their best jokes were usually at the expense of Friends themselves.

In this Yearly Meeting of 1858 the voices which usually spoke in gently ironical asides began to ring out in open criticism. A new spirit was stirring in the Society. There were a good many Friends who had begun to doubt whether the preservation of *all* their time-honoured customs might not be, in fact, more pig-headed obstinacy than a true interpretation of the ancient light by which their forefathers had walked.

The question of 'plain dress' came up again for discussion, and it is clear from young Joseph Rowntree's notes that he himself took sides with those who thought that the rule about this should be changed or abolished.

'Samuel Sturge', he records, 'made a queer speech in favour of things as they are. But it is always pleasant to hear him, he is such a spirited old man.'

Thomas Satterthwaite, on the other hand, said that if Friends persisted in their present practice there would soon be no one but the silver-haired and infirm to conduct the business of the Society; and William Thistlethwaite pointed out that religion led to simplicity, not to a costume.

The question of 'plain dress' was also finally referred to a committee, and three years later, when the Book of Discipline was revised, the paragraph concerning 'plainness' was omitted. Thereafter the clothes which Friends wore were no longer a matter of public concern to the Society—though private criticism probably continued. 'Thee dresses thy children in a very *bright* drab,' was the reproach made to one woman Friend some time after this, and one of the children still remembered it in 1945.

The abolition of the rule did not change Friends' taste for clothes which were rich in material and simple in style. Photographs of Quaker women in the seventies and eighties generally show them in plain full-skirted dark dresses, when the fashion of the day was an 'orgy of frills and flounces, loops, draperies, cascades, chutes and ondulations'. Men like the elder Joseph continued to wear the coats without lapels which they had worn all their lives. It is a tribute to their perspicacity and open-mindedness that it was *they* who struggled to get the rule changed; and thereby relieved the younger members of the Society from restrictions which had been to many of them a real stumbling-block.

Altogether the Yearly Meeting of 1858 showed signs of growth and change in the Society which must have been encouraging to all except the most crusted die-hards. Certainly the elder Joseph travelled back to York in a more hopeful frame of mind than he had done in 1857. Some of the depression from which he had suffered for many years began to lift; and in the autumn, when his fellow-councillors unanimously elected him Mayor of York, he was 'much touched by this token of their esteem'.

But he refused the honour. He had seen it coming and he knew what he had to say. He referred to the office of Mayor as that of the 'Chief Magistrate of the City,' and he declined it because of its 'connection with the administration of oaths'.

There was applause when he finished speaking. Perhaps his fellow-councillors considered him a little eccentric, but there is no doubt that they both liked and respected him.

The elder Joseph probably felt few regrets for the pomp and importance of the office he had refused. He was only fifty-seven, but he was beginning to feel himself an old man. He had worked very hard at more things than business all his life, and now he was looking for opportunities to 'pass his responsibilities on to other shoulders'. The shop in Pavement was left more and more in the hands of his sons, and although he went down to it almost every day he no longer dined there with the apprentices.

John, the eldest son, had taken charge of the Pavement 'family' when he was twenty-one, going to live in the old rooms over the shop and acting as head of the household. In the summer of 1858 he married Elizabeth Hotham, and she took on the tasks which had once been Sarah Rowntree's—the running of the unwieldy establishment and the mothering of the young apprentices. The elder Joseph admired his first daughter-in-law, and evidently felt quite content to leave the domestic side of the Pavement business in her hands, only urging her 'not to spare trouble, *or even cost*, in thy arrangements for the comfort of the young men'.

He had still felt responsible for the boys who came to work for him, but after John's marriage he gave up a custom more than thirty years' old—that of reading aloud to the apprentices on Sunday evenings. He was apparently satisfied that John and Elizabeth would look after the spiritual as well as the material needs of those under their roof.

The elder Joseph died on November 4, 1859. The Mayor and Corporation followed the funeral procession to the Friends' burial-ground; and all the shops in Pavement and Walmgate, as well as many others, were closed as a sign of respect.

Fifty-eight is not a great age, but the elder Joseph died feeling that his work had been done. And indeed he left very few loose threads behind him. His long struggle with the Society of Friends over the Marriage Regulations had succeeded six months before his death. The boys' school in York which he had helped to establish was flourishing. The girls' school had been nursed—financially and in other ways—through a move to new and healthier premises. His sons were established in life and his widow was comfortably settled in a handsome house. It was no small achievement for the young man who had come to York when he was twenty-one with 'little capital except his ability, industry, and integrity'.

Young Joseph was twenty-three when his father died, and John was twenty-five. The whole management of the Pavement business now devolved on them, and they had their mother and sister to support, as well as John's wife. There was enough money to go round, but not a great deal to spare. And the young men had inherited also many of their father's other responsibilities. John became secretary to the Management Committee of the two Friends' Schools, and Joseph took his father's place on the same Committee. He also followed his father as co-manager of the British School in Hope Street, which was then the only undenominational school in York.

All this, with Adult School teaching on Sundays, made up a full programme for the two young men. Nevertheless Joseph managed to do his courting at this time, though he generally had to go to Bradford and later to Luton tó meet Julia Seebohm. Sometimes she came to York with her parents for a Quarterly Meeting, but on these occasions the two young people were under the observant gaze of a formidable array of relations and Friends, and it was almost impossible for them to meet and talk unremarked. It was probably easier when the Seebohms came to Harrogate—as they did for a few weeks nearly every summer—and certainly by some means Julia and Joseph managed to keep their feelings hidden from their families until they became formally engaged eight months before their marriage. It is unlikely that there would have been any sort of parental opposition, since the friendship between the Seebohms and the Rowntrees was of such long standing, but probably Joseph wished to be left alone to manage his affairs in his own way—not always an easy business in a Society as closely united as that of nineteenth-century Friends.

Julia's parents moved in 1861 from Bradford to Luton, where their younger son was living. Another son was established at Hitchin, and it was in the Friends' Meeting House in this town that Joseph and Julia were married on the August 15, 1862.

Esther Seebohm, in the flowery language of the day, described her daughter's wedding in her memorandum book.

'Julia left the parental home with her best-beloved J.R. . . . Her little bark is not laden with silver and gold, but richly freight with the love and kindness of her friends. She goes out possessed of a husband worthy of her, and into the bosom of a dear Christian family.'

Julia married, rather literally, into the bosom of the Rowntrees; for she and Joseph set up housekeeping in part of his mother's house at the corner of Bootham and St. Mary's. They had their own front door on Bootham, but from their basement kitchen to their servants' rooms on the top storey there was a connecting door or passage to Sarah Rowntree's house on every floor.

It was a curious establishment. Sarah Rowntree, who was of a practical turn of mind, and had had years of experience of difficult kitchens from the Pavement house onwards, had taken a revolutionary step for the times in which she lived. She had moved her kitchen up from the basement when Joseph married, and divided her enormous drawing-room in half. Part of it she turned into a dining-room for herself, and the rest became a sitting-room for Julia and Joseph. She established her own kitchen in what had once been her dining-room and made one of the big bedrooms on the first floor into a drawing-room.

Julia and Joseph were given the vast original kitchen in the basement, with a coal cellar and a larder and a scullery thrown in. They had a sitting-room on the ground floor, two bedrooms above it, and three servants' rooms at the top of the house. They had their own flights of stairs to all four levels, but even so it must have been a situation full of potential difficulties. The fact that none appear to have arisen is a tribute to Sarah, who was always a woman of discretion in her personal relationships. She did not intrude on the young people, though they generally went through to her house on Sundays, either for midday dinner or for tea. It may even have been a comfort to Julia to have such an old friend as her mother-in-law near at hand. Her domestic duties were light, for she had two maids, and Joseph dined with the apprentices at Pavement in the middle of the day. But he rarely came home before seven in the evening, and it was a long day for a girl to get through alone. Perhaps Julia was glad to be able to run in and out of the big Rowntree house next door, where her sister-in-law Hannah Rowntree, who was only a year older than herself, was still living. The two young women took together the 'little turns in the garden' which Joseph was constantly urging on his wife. He thought that she spent too much time indoors, and that fresh air would improve her health. In fact he was gently bracing with her and discouraged her from sitting too long over the fire.

Julia had never been strong and she became pregnant as soon as she was married. She probably felt unwell for much of that first year of her marriage, and a photograph of her with her husband shows a rather solemn face, though she is described as being 'direct of speech and gay in manner'.

Certainly she cannot have lacked friends in York, for many of her contemporaries at the Mount School were now living in the city, and perhaps she was happy enough, in spite of her health, during the months while she waited for her baby to be born. It is to be hoped so, for she did not live to see another winter.

Julia and Joseph's daughter was born on May 30, 1863. They called her Julia Seebohm Rowntree, but her pet name became 'Lilley'. Joseph was always fond of young children, and this first baby of his own must have been a great joy to him. He sent his family away, however, to Scarborough in August, for his wife had made a slow recovery from her confinement and he hoped that she might benefit from the change of air.

Julia enjoyed Scarborough, and her health seemed to improve a little. But at the end of August she returned to York and almost immediately she became suddenly and desperately ill. Joseph sent for her mother, who reached York on September 4th. It was clear to Esther Seebohm that her daughter's condition was extremely serious. She wrote at once to her husband, who was in Germany visiting his relations, and Benjamin replied with a letter about Christian trials and consolations which cannot have been much comfort to his wife. Nor did he, as might have been expected, start for England even after he received a second and even more ominous letter from York. His confidence in his daughter's state of 'Christian preparedness' for death may have sustained his own courage, but his wife would probably have been glad of his presence to help her through the two dreadful weeks in which her only daughter lay dying. He reached York at last, a few hours after Julia's death.

She died on September 21st, and the death certificate gives the cause of death as 'congestion of the brain'. It was probably what would now be called meningitis.

CHAPTER SEVEN

UNTIL Julia died most things had gone well for Joseph throughout his twenty-seven years. He had had a happy childhood, and an adolescence less rebellious than that of many young men, thanks to his father's tolerance and understanding. Although he had had to take on a good deal of responsibility at an early age, he had not been unprepared for it. Several times before he was twenty-three he was left in sole charge of the Pavement shop for a week or more. Julia's death, at the age of twenty-two, was his first encounter with tragedy.

The sudden onslaught of his wife's last illness must have been a shock to Joseph. No doubt he had worried about her when the baby was born, for in those days childbirth was a dangerous business, but she had survived her confinement and had appeared to be slowly recovering her strength. She had been well enough to go away with the baby for a holiday. Then, without warning, she had collapsed, and a fortnight later she was dead. Joseph was left, after thirteen months of marriage, alone with a three-months'-old daughter.

On the practical level everything was soon arranged. Joseph's sister Hannah came through one of those connecting doors from his mother's house to live with him and look after 'Lilley'. She was a devoted aunt, and the baby grew and flourished under her care. Even so his house must have been a lonely place for the young widower, and for several years it was his habit to stay at the Pavement shop until very late in the evening. All his personal letters in these years are headed '28 The Pavement'. He must have sat writing them in the counting-house, with the darkened empty shop beyond, until at last he could no longer put off going home to those rooms in Bootham.

In the spring after Julia's death Joseph took a holiday, and spent four weeks in France and Switzerland. His cousin Joshua

Rowntree went with him, and including their fares the holiday cost them twenty-six pounds five and sixpence each. Joseph notes in his account book that this was an average of 16/11½ a day. It was probably money well spent, for Joseph had never been abroad before, and his first visit to Switzerland—a country which he came to love in later life—must have been at least a distraction.

He found, presently, another mild consolation. He began to collect statistics about poverty.

This preoccupation with the unfortunate condition of a million of his countrymen was not a new thing. It had begun, long ago, with that visit to Ireland; and later, teaching in the Adult School, he had pursued the subject unobtrusively in conversations with his pupils. Now, restless and lonely, he set himself to work out his conclusions.

It was a time when the social conscience was beginning to stir all over the country, and the full force of the Industrial Revolution was at last becoming apparent even to those who had no direct contact with industry. For more than two generations people had been steadily moving away from the countryside and into the towns, and the cholera epidemics of 1848–49 and of 1854 had exposed some of the horrors of town life: the drinking water brown with sewage; the single rooms where a family of twelve slept, ate, and accomplished their births and deaths; the gin shops in which even five-year-old children could be seen seeking oblivion at a penny a glass.

These things, by the time Joseph started to tabulate his figures, were beginning to trouble even some people who had recently believed that the 'lowly path' of the poor had been allotted to them by God and should not be altered by man. All but the most complacent observer could now see that some of the burdens of poverty were too heavy for anyone to carry. And Joseph was not at all complacent. Nor did he make the general Victorian distinction between the 'respectable' poor and the rest. He treated the whole question scientifically, and his wide range of statistics, collected for analysis and comparison, are the work of a pioneer. They have little in common with the usual philanthropic activity of the day, and are as far removed from the 'soup kitchen' started by his father in York as from the coals and blankets given by a good squire's wife to her cottage tenants.

It was characteristic of Joseph, even at twenty-seven, that he was not tempted into any hasty or dramatic action. He assembled his facts slowly and carefully, looking always for the root cause behind the present misery. He traced back the history of the English Poor Laws for five hundred years, to the time of the Black Death. The Poor Laws, however, turned out to be only part of the story. Too much of the country's wealth was being spent on armaments, he found, and a ludicrously small amount on education. One thing leads to another. In those first solitary months after Julia's death, Joseph prepared not only statistics of the number of paupers in England during the past twelve years, but also tables to illustrate the number of illiterate men and women in the country. He got his figures from the marriage registers, which showed how many people could sign their names and how many simply made a 'mark'. There was a connection—at least in Joseph's own mind—between poverty and illiteracy and crime. He worked out the statistics of crime from the year 1805 to the year 1860. The economic factor was part of the whole complex problem, so he undertook to analyse the export and import figures, the national expenditure, the details of population, and the 'division of classes'.

For the last estimate he took his figures from the Custom and Excise Authorities, who classified the population of their time as follows:

'One million   .. Upper and Wealthy.
Nine million   .. Merchants' Clerks, Shopkeepers, etc.
Eighteen million .. Mechanics and Operatives.
One million   .. Poor.'

The implications behind that bland statement were not lost on Joseph.

His tables of statistics remain clear and unfaded still, after nearly a hundred years, the figures emphasized here and there with red ink instead of black, the lines drawn thick and straight on the heavy blue paper; and the strength of his feeling also remains undimmed. When he had compiled his figures he wrote an essay, and it was called 'British Civilization. In what it consists. And in what it does *not* consist'.

This paper was designed to be read to a conference of Adult School Teachers, and he did read portions of it, both at Leeds and at Bristol, during the year 1864. It was necessary, however, to tone them down slightly.

J. Storrs Fry, who was arranging the Bristol conference, wrote after reading the essay, that he 'wished to avoid any cause of offence to weak brethren, which the truth does not *necessarily* involve', and he queries whether Joseph's language is not 'a little too strong in places'.

'We must look *soberly* at stern facts,' he adds.

Joseph was not, at this moment, in the mood to look at his facts with anything except horror. His manuscript shows where he made cuts—but there were not many of them. The 'weak brethren' had to make the best they could of it. They had some touches of humour to help them on, though even Joseph's jokes reflected the strength of his indignation. He quotes, in the section of his essay dealing with crime, the summing-up of a judge at Stafford, delivering judgement some fifty years earlier. The prisoner was convicted of uttering a forged note, value one pound, and the judge condemned him to death, exhorted him to prepare himself for a better world, and added, 'And I trust that through the mediation of our blessed Redeemer, you may *there* experience that mercy which a *proper regard* for the paper currency of the country forbids you to hope for *here*'.

In 1865 Joseph wrote another essay. It was shorter and more specialized than the earlier one on 'British Civilization'. There were fewer quotations in it—and before being publicly delivered it had to be cut much more drastically than its predecessors. It was called 'Pauperism in England and Wales'.

Joseph was thirty now, and the diffidence of his youth had largely disappeared. He had been assembling his facts from many sources for nearly half his life—from reading, from conversation with men of all classes, from observing the customers in his shop. In this essay on 'Pauperism' it is a man's voice, calm and assured, which sounds through the cool historical dissection of the Poor Laws, compares various systems of indoor and outdoor relief, and discusses technicalities concerned with the Law of Removal. And when he passes from the particular to the general his sentences ring out, not with the passionate indignation of a young man, but with the measured authority of someone who is certain of his position.

'The Medical Officer of the Board of Health has recently declared, after most careful investigation, that one-fifth of our population have not a sufficiency of food and clothing. It is a monstrous thing that in this land, rich in natural wealth and now rich beyond all precedent, millions of its inhabitants, made in the image of their Creator, should spend their days in a struggle for existence so severe as to blight (where it does not destroy) the higher parts of their nature. . . .'

Most of the blame for all this, in Joseph's opinion, lay at the doors of the Church and the State. They were the 'gigantic obstacles in the path'. Their social ideals were framed exclusively upon the precedents of the past.

'They are willing for the people to be happy—*if* that happiness can co-exist with their exclusive privileges. . . . But when we turn to Christianity as the only radical cure for the sorrows of nations and of men, we find that one half of the organized Christian life of this country is paralysed by its connection with the State. When the voice of British Christianity should make itself heard—when there is a massacre in Jamaica or an Opium War in China—when public opinion is faltering upon the question of Negro Slavery—the twenty thousand clergymen of the Church of England are silent. . . . They only recover their power of speech when the interests of their order are assailed, and do not hesitate, for instance, to arrest the civilization of Ireland. . . .'

Someone, not, I think, J. Storrs Fry this time, had to ask Joseph to modify his paper. It was too strong meat even for Friends. But, in the light of events still far in the future, one sentence which was *not* cut deserves recording.

63

'Charity as ordinarily practised, the charity of endowment, the charity of emotion, the charity which takes the place of justice, creates much of the misery which it relieves, but does not relieve all the misery it creates.'

Nearly forty years later, when he set up three Trusts with the great fortune which he had earned, Joseph's instructions to his Trustees showed that his feelings were still the same. He wished the money to be used in ways which might serve to expose the root causes of poverty, and not to be spent relieving 'obvious distress or evil, which generally evoke so much feeling that the necessary agencies for alleviating them are pretty adequately supported'.

Joseph, wrestling with figures and writing fiery denunciations of Church and State, was fortunate in that his own position was more or less unassailable. There were many criticisms which could be made of Friends and their ways, but on the whole it was undeniable that they practised what they preached. They really tried to carry their code of ethics into every corner of their lives; to connect the teaching of the gospels with the practical business of a household or a shop. Naturally they did not always succeed; but they managed well enough to make it almost impossible for anyone to denounce them as Joseph denounced the Established Church.

Joseph's faith in the Society of Friends was deep and sure. He knew the Quaker weaknesses. His father had been openly gloomy and doubtful for years about the state of the Society; and his brother John had published an essay in 1858 on the 'causes of the decline in the Society of Friends' which contained criticisms of an extremely trenchant sort. Joseph himself criticized Friends from time to time, but his faith in the general rightness of their beliefs was never shaken. He very seldom, at any period in his life, spoke of his own religious convictions. They can only be deduced from passages marked in some much-read books. And one letter, written to his mother-in-law two months after Julia's death, contains the sentences: 'I cannot but believe that the spirits of my Father and my Wife are *even now* engaged in the high and holy

At school in 1848—Joseph on the extreme left, Henry Isaac extreme right

2 Joseph Rowntree and his first wife, 1862

Joseph Rowntree in 1868, the year he joined his brother Henry Isaac

Joseph Rowntree at 42 years of age

3 The Rowntree shop in Pavement before rebuilding

services of Heaven. I am at present quite unable to meet what Whately says in favour of the soul passing into a state of *perfect unconsciousness* at the moment of death. . . . I shrink with horror from the thought of a practical annihilation for (it may be) thousands of years, and to have to picture our darling not as in Heaven but as in the tomb. Does thou, or does Papa, know any work which gives the scriptural argument on the other side?'

Esther Seebohm probably replied comfortingly. She was a woman to whom grief was nothing new. As long as she lived— which was only a year longer than her daughter—she and her son-in-law remained on terms of affection and intimacy.

Joseph had, also, friends nearer his own age to help him through these years. Joshua Rowntree, the cousin with whom he had gone abroad, was now articled to a solicitor in York, and the two often met and walked together to their places of business in the morning. They had many interests in common, and when Joshua went to London in 1865 he wrote long and racy letters to Joseph in York.

'You've a great responsibility in the North,' one of these letters runs, 'for it's manifest the deliverance of the Society must come from there. *Here* we are still in the Middle Ages.'

The same letter ends with a mildly funny story about a 'popular hireling priest'. The writer excuses it by saying he never likes to omit '*some* allusion to the State church'.

So, with statistics as a bulwark against despair, with hard work, good friends, and a true faith in God, Joseph got through the years of his widowerhood. He kept in very close touch with the Seebohms, even after the death of his mother-in-law. Frederic and Henry, Julia's brothers, had both been schoolfellows of his at Bootham; and now when he went to London he often visited Hitchin and stayed a night or two with Frederic.

These Seebohm brothers both had the Quaker habit of following a hobby quite unconnected with the things by which they earned their living. It was, however, rather unusual for such part-time occupations to make a man famous. But both Henry and Frederic became in their time authorities on their chosen subjects. Henry, whose business was iron and steel, was a well-known naturalist and the author of a number of authoritative books on English and Eastern birds. When he died at the age of sixty-seven he left over one hundred thousand pounds, a fortune made entirely by himself, and also a notable ornithological collection to the British Museum.

Frederic's profession was banking, but he achieved distinction as an economic historian. In his day he was *the* expert on the primitive system of land tenure in Britain and the open-field method of agriculture. But he also published books on subjects as diverse as the Black Death and compulsory education. At the same time he was a very successful banker. Such a career was still possible in the days before the technician and the specialist became the rulers of life.

It was at Frederic's house, and in the winter of 1867, that Joseph met Emma Antoinette Seebohm. She was the daugher of Wilhelm Seebohm of Hamburg, and a first cousin of Joseph's dead wife; a slight girl with silvery fair hair, who was not quite twenty-one when she first came to England.

Benjamin Seebohm's wool business in Bradford had not been a successful venture. Nevertheless, while he was engaged in it, he exported a good deal of wool to Germany. At Friedensthal his brother John managed a wool-sorting or 'accommodating' business, to which Benjamin sent his goods; and from the same place two other brothers, Wilhelm and August, established branches in Hamburg and Dusseldorf. Emma Antoinette was Wilhelm's daughter. He sent her to stay with her cousins at Hitchin in the autumn of 1866, to spend some months learning English.

Joseph was a familiar visitor in this Seebohm household, but perhaps Frederic and his wife noticed that this winter his visits were more frequent than usual. In the spring he attended Yearly Meeting in London, and afterwards he went again to Hitchin. Emma Antoinette was still there. For one reason or another her return to Hamburg had been postponed.

In August Joseph proposed to her. He wrote to Julia's father: 'Thou will perhaps have heard that I went to Hitchin on 4th day, spending the night at Fred's, and that Tonie then gave me the answer I so much desired. . . . It is peculiarly grateful to me that in being engaged it should be to one who is so dear to thee and so dear to you all; and who seems to fill our hearts so much more than anyone could have been expected to fill, the place of darling Julie.'

Emma Antoinette, whom the family called Tonie, probably did not realize then how difficult it was going to be for her to take Julia's place. In fact it could not be done. Joseph and Julia had been friends from their schooldays. That particular youthful relationship, with all its family links and its shared inheritance of childish jokes and memories, could never be repeated. Antoinette had to make her own history, and it must have been an uphill task. In those early days of her marriage she must have often felt that she was, in fact, only an echo of the dead girl she had never known.

They were married in the Meeting House at Hitchin, as Julia and Joseph had been on November 14, 1867. They spent three weeks in Devonshire and Herefordshire, and then returned to York, to the house which had been Julia's, and to the child of four and a half who bore her name.

Antoinette, unlike Julia, had not been familiar with the Rowntrees all her life. She may very well have found them rather overpowering. There was her mother-in-law in the house next door with all those connecting passages on every storey, and also her brother-in-law, Henry Isaac. Her other brother-in-law, John, had moved from the Pavement shop-house in 1865, and was established at Mount Villas with his wife and five children. There were more Rowntrees at Scarborough, and at Settrington, and at Malton. And Antoinette was still more or less a stranger in a strange land. It cannot have been an easy situation for her; and she was responsible, as well, for a stepdaughter who was a delicate and probably a slightly spoiled child (her father refers to her 'giving directions with her usual air') and who no doubt missed the aunt who had been her constant companion for as long as she could remember. Fortunately Hannah was not now living in the other part of the house. She had married George Gillet a month before Antoinette married Joseph.

These early years set their mark on Joseph's second wife, and they may account for some of the quirks in her character as she grew older. Hers was never a naturally happy disposition, and perhaps she lived for too long on the defensive, suspecting that her in-laws were comparing her with her predecessor, wondering if they were criticizing her dealings with her stepchild, very much aware of the memories left by that cousin who had died so tragically that no one ever spoke of her except with love and pity.

Joseph was an indulgent husband to Antoinette. Julia's death had shaken his faith in women's stamina. He no longer urged the advantages of fresh air and exercise, and he was more anxious about the birth of his second child than he had been about his first.

But John Wilhelm was born safely on September 4, 1868; and Antoinette, in a photograph taken with him when he was a few months old, looks delighted with her flourishing baby.

In the year after his son's birth Joseph left the shop in Pavement where he had worked since he was an apprentice, and joined his younger brother, Henry Isaac, who now owned a 'Cocoa, Chocolate and Chicory Works' at Tanner's Moat, down by the river.

For Joseph it must have been a great change. All his life had been bound up with the shop in Pavement. He had been born there, most of his childhood had been spent there, and he had worked there for seventeen years. The counting-house had been his refuge, as it was his father's before him. Now everything was different.

But there was one more change to come; one last connection with his early life to be broken. In April that year, his daughter 'Lilley' had a bad sore throat. She was ill for a month before Caleb Williams, an old and much-loved Quaker doctor who had attended Joseph's father, pronounced that she had scarlet fever. A week later she was dead.

For Joseph this grief had a double edge. He was devoted to the child, and knew her much more intimately than most fathers of that day knew their children. He had taken some of the domestic

68

responsibility for her which would, in the normal course of events, have been her mother's. And she had been the last tangible link with his 'darling Julie'.

There was anxiety as well as sorrow in the household, for the baby John Wilhelm was only eight months old, and everyone feared that he might have caught scarlet fever from 'Lilley'. Fortunately, however, he escaped the infection, and presently Joseph was able to send his wife and baby away for a change of air. He himself stayed in York, and perhaps welcomed the demands made upon his time and energy by the new business he was learning. Now, in the mornings, he walked down to Lendal Bridge and across the river to Tanner's Moat, instead of under Bootham Bar and through the city to Pavement. It was a change which marked the end of an epoch in his life.

CHAPTER EIGHT

MANY large business undertakings have a history of small beginnings, but not many can trace their origin back to a woman's enterprise. Yet there is an unbroken connection between the modern firm of Rowntree & Co. and a little grocer's shop which Mary Tuke opened in Walmgate in the year 1725.

Mary Tuke was a Quaker, the daughter of a blacksmith, and a girl of courage and character. She was orphaned when young, and at thirty she was still unmarried. She decided to go into business.

Perhaps there was some head-shaking over this example of female independence, but Mary was the eldest of the family and none of her relatives appear to have had sufficient authority to prevent her doing as she pleased. Obviously she was a difficult creature to intimidate, for even the Merchant Adventurers' Company of the city of York never managed to exact the fines they imposed on her for trading without a licence. The Company claimed the right of a monopoly in all dealings in matters 'foreign bought and foreign sold', and it could empower people by licence to carry on such dealings within the city. But a licence cost money, and no doubt Mary Tuke had very little to spare when she first opened her shop.

For five years the struggle between Mary and the Merchant Adventurers was fought with obstinacy on one side and a certain amount of chivalry on the other. The Company ordered her to be prosecuted, gave her six months to dispose of her shop goods, and constantly summoned her to appear before their court. But —somehow or other—they never managed to make her shut her shop. Perhaps they were only concerned to preserve some semblance of their own dignity, and were too genuinely kind-hearted to drive an enterprising woman out of business. At any rate the little grocer's shop remained open, and even when Mary married Henry Frankland, a 'stuff-weaver', she did not abandon her own trade. In fact, soon after their marriage her husband left his job and joined her in the shop. He, in turn, came into collision with the Merchant Adventurers; but there was now some money available, and everything was much easier. In due course he paid his admission fee and was given the 'Freedom of the Fellowship', thus becoming a member of the Company.

Mary was left a childless widow at the age of forty-four. She took her nephew, William Tuke, as an apprentice; and when she died, in 1752, she left him all her property.

William Tuke was only twenty at this time, but after some hesitation he decided to carry on the shop by himself. It had been moved from Walmgate during Mary's lifetime, and was now established in Castlegate. And there it still remained when young Henry Isaac Rowntree joined the firm over a hundred years later.

In those hundred years, after a lean beginning, the Tukes had prospered. William Tuke lived to be eighty-seven, and in the course of his long life the grocer's shop became a more specialized affair. Tuke & Co. became Tea Dealers, and presently Chocolate and Cocoa Manufacturers. Outside his business William Tuke became known as the founder of The Retreat, a 'habitation for persons in a state of lunacy', where chains and stripes were abolished and a revolutionary system of kindness towards the insane was established.

For three generations the management of Tuke & Co. descended from father to son; but in 1857, when Samuel Tuke died, neither of his sons returned to York to take over the shop and factory in Castlegate. One had become a partner in a bank at Hitchin, and the other was running a branch of Tuke's which he had established in London. In York there was only a manager, Henry Hipsley, who was a family connection of the Tukes, but never became a partner.

Samuel Tuke and the elder Joseph Rowntree were lifelong friends. Perhaps, before Samuel became too ill to look after his business, he may have indicated to Joseph that there was a profitable opening in it for one of the Rowntree boys, since his own sons showed no wish to be responsible for the firm in York.

Henry Isaac Rowntree went to work for the Tukes in 1860, after he had served his apprenticeship in his father's shop. He had not been made a partner in the grocery business, as his two elder brothers had been on their twenty-first birthdays, so it is reasonable to assume that his patrimony was given to him in some other form. Perhaps the elder Joseph bought for his youngest son some kind of financial interest in the firm to which he moved. Certainly in 1862, three years after the elder Joseph's death, Henry Isaac was in a position to buy the cocoa and chocolate-making department of Tuke & Co.

The change of business was announced as follows:

'We have to inform you that we have relinquished the manufacture of Cocoa, Chocolate and Chicory in favour of our friend, H. I. Rowntree, who has been for some time practically engaged on the concern, and whose knowledge of the business in its several departments enables us with confidence to recommend him to the notice of our connection.

'We remain very respectfully,
'Tuke and Company,
'York. 1st of 7th Month 1862.'

A circular was enclosed with this announcement, and in it Henry Isaac informs his customers that by the introduction of 'new and improved machinery' he is prepared to execute promptly any orders with which he may be favoured.

'Tuke's Superior Rock Cocoa' was much esteemed in the neighbourhood of York. It sold for ninepence a pound wholesale, and was a blend of pure cocoa and sugar, compressed into a sort of cake. This cocoa, subsequently renamed Rowntree's Prize Medal Rock Cocoa after it had won a medal at a local exhibition, was the main product of the factory for which Henry Isaac became responsible soon after his twenty-fourth birthday. 'Homœopathic cocoa', which had arrowroot added to it, was also manufactured and sold in powder form in packets, but Rock cocoa was the foundation of the business. Henry Isaac, who was a witty and light-hearted young man, often quoted the thirty-first verse of the thirty-second chapter of Deuteronomy in its praise. 'For their Rock is not as our Rock, even our enemies themselves being judges.'

Nevertheless, excellent though Prize Medal Rock Cocoa was, Henry Isaac could not make enough profit out of it to finance the extension of his business. There are no accurate records of the yearly output of his factory before 1870, but in the year 1862 his total sales were estimated as under £3,000. Perhaps it was unwise of him, in these circumstances, to buy not only a 'wonderful new machine' for grinding cocoa, but also a collection of buildings for which he paid £1,000. These buildings were an old iron foundry, several cottages, and a tavern, all close together down by the river. On one side ran the little street called Tanner's Moat, and it was by this name that Henry Isaac's factory came to be known after he moved it from the original premises in Castlegate.

By modern standards it was hardly a factory at all. It employed no more than a dozen men and its output was about twelve hundredweight of cocoa a week. As time went on Henry Isaac had a hard struggle to keep the business going. By 1869, seven years after he had bought the business from Tuke & Co., he found himself in a position of some difficulty.

It was at this point that Joseph joined his younger brother, taking his capital out of the Pavement shop and putting it into the business at Tanner's Moat. The Rowntrees were bred in the old tradition of family responsibility, and it was sufficiently compelling to cause Joseph, in this case, to learn a new trade when he was already thirty-three years old.

In all trades, however, there is one constant factor—the accounts. It was this side of the business which Joseph took over, leaving Henry Isaac to deal with the actual manufacture of the cocoa.

'Time and Motion Study' had not been invented and costing systems were still in their infancy, but one of the things Joseph really knew about was statistics. As he had once worked out figures of national expenditure with regard to pauperism, so now he began to explore the costs of producing the various kinds of cocoa. A boy who worked with him, in that first year at Tanner's Moat, remembered long afterwards his accuracy and his meticulous attention to small details. His was the scientific approach to every problem, whether it was the poverty of his countrymen or the sale of his brother's cocoa, and it proved of very great value to the business.

It is difficult, in this age of specialization, to understand how simply a factory such as Tanner's Moat was conducted in the seventies. Even when the number of employees rose to thirty, there was little distinction between the 'office' and the 'factory' staff. Joseph was very particular about handwriting—he himself taught it in the Adult School—and he often set a young man the task of copying out lists of different sorts for a fortnight before he was allowed to start his real work in the office. But the chief thing required of everyone was that they should be able-bodied. When there was need for it the 'office' staff had to help carry sacks of cocoa and sugar.

'What can you do?' Joseph would ask the applicant for a job. 'Can you carry a ten-stone bag of flour?'

If the answer was in the affirmative the next question was usually, 'When can you start?'

The system of payment was very simple. Each employee kept his own time, and at the end of the week the general foreman, a man called Hanks, went round with a hat full of silver and copper asking everyone in turn, 'How much time has thee got?' Sometimes, if the cash did not balance against his own account, he was obliged to go round again enquiring, '*What* did I give thee?' It was all very friendly and uncomplicated.

In his private office, which was a pleasant room with an end window looking over Lendal bridge, Joseph's own arrangements were simple, too. He had a trap-door in the floor beside his desk, and if he wished to speak to anyone in the counting-house which was below his room he pulled up the trap-door and called the man's name. Urgent letters for the post were also dropped through this trap-door, with the request that someone should take them over the bridge to the Post Office. This was often followed by the remark, 'And buy me six penny rock buns at Terry's, too, please.'

Tanner's Moat, in those early days, was much nearer in spirit to an eighteenth-century workshop than to the great modern factory which was to grow out of it. There was a parrot in one of the workrooms, and a temperamental donkey in the stables, who was given a Turkish bath from time to time by means of steam pipes run from the factory. The donkey was used to deliver orders in the city, but when its particular attendant left the factory it kicked everyone else so fiercely that it had to be sold, and the local deliveries in future were done by a hand-cart. It was a world where domesticity still impinged upon industrialism, where cocoa and pork-pies were provided by Joseph and Henry Isaac on nights when men had to work overtime, where wet coats were dried on hot pipes in the 'roasting' department, and where each man had a coherent idea of the business as a whole.

Joseph may have gone to Tanner's Moat with a certain amount of misgiving, but it was not long before he began to feel about the place as he had felt about the Pavement shop, that it was his own world and that the men who worked in it were his 'family'. He knew them all as well as his father had known the apprentices who were part of the Pavement household. No one at Tanner's Moat, in those first years, could have fallen ill or run into any sort of domestic or financial trouble without Joseph or Henry Isaac hearing something about it. And this was a time when every workman 'had a pistol pointed at his heart'. Any change in fashion, even a bad harvest in a land whose name he did not know, could throw a man out of employment and bring disaster on his family.

There was no system of State insurance against unemployment, sickness, or old age. Friendly societies, Trade Unions, and industrial insurance companies were the means by which the 'respectable' poor tried to ward off calamity. The less respectable poor did not even try; they knew it was hopeless. But even the most provident and thrifty could not possibly, out of their small income, insure themselves against *all* the risks which were an inescapable part of their lives. For most of them there were few safeguards except such as might lie in the character and capability of their employer.

But the Rowntree brothers had not forgotten the tradition in which they were reared, and the men who worked for them felt comparatively secure. It was said in York that 'Rowntrees look after their people'.

In return Joseph and Henry Isaac got good service; and the sort of loyal, almost fanatical interest which is perhaps only possible in a small concern where each individual can *see* his own work in relation to everyone else's. Yet, in spite of general hard work, in spite of Joseph's reorganization and Henry Isaac's enthusiasm, it took nearly ten years to make any real commercial progress. This may have been due, in part, to a general trade depression, for prices fell steadily from 1873 to 1879, and both English farming and English industries were beginning to feel the effect of foreign competition.

Meanwhile, in these years, Joseph's domestic responsibilities increased. John Wilhelm, the eldest Rowntree boy, was not a year old when Joseph first went to Tanner's Moat, and a daughter, Agnes Julia, was born in 1870. Another son, Benjamin Seebohm, who was always called Seebohm, was born in 1871. It is a little strange that both on Agnes's and Seebohm's birth certificates, Joseph still describes himself as a 'Master Grocer'. It was only in 1875, when his third son was born, that he called himself a 'cocoa manufacturer'. Had he, perhaps, some faint hope of eventually returning to the shop in Pavement? Or was it simply a slip of the pen?

Joseph's home, since his first marriage, had been in Bootham —the part of his mother's house which had been converted for him in 1862. When there were three babies it was definitely overcrowded, as well as being thoroughly unworkable from a domestic point of view. It had only one sitting-room and two family bedrooms. An extra room was 'borrowed' from Joseph's mother as the family increased, but even so it cannot have been a very comfortable arrangement for anyone. By the spring of 1875, when

Joseph's wife was pregnant with her fourth child, it was obvious that a move would have to be made.

The family did not go very far; only, in fact, across the road. Joseph rented from Bootham School a house which the Committee owned next door to the school buildings. It was then Number Nineteen, Bootham, and is now the Headmaster's house, a comfortable eighteenth-century building with well-proportioned rooms and graceful windows. Joseph paid the school seventy pounds a year for this house, and lived in it for the next seven years.

Joseph's wife should now have found her life much easier than it had been in the cramped quarters which were part of her mother-in-law's house. But Antoinette was not a woman who found life easy in any circumstances. She was a worrier. She fretted over John Wilhelm's toothaches and Seebohm's 'pasty appearance'. She had not been born a Friend, though she joined the Society soon after her marriage, and she never acquired that passionage preoccupation with Quaker affairs which had made life so full of incident for earlier generations of Quaker women. She never had much enthusiasm for the business of Monthly or Quarterly Meetings; and she did not become deeply enough involved in the life of the Society to undertake those pleasant journeys about the country which had provided social distraction as well as spiritual exercise for her husband's mother and grandmother. She must, I think, have found her existence often very dull. She had married into the Rowntree clan and the Society of Friends, and theirs was still a world where the ordinary pleasures of the ordinary woman had no standing. Clothes were unfashionable and plain, dancing was unthinkable, music perhaps not *harmful* but certainly frivolous, and social occasions consisted chiefly of entertaining travelling Friends and relations.

Antoinette, with her silvery fair hair parted in the middle, and a noticeably erect way of standing or sitting, was a young woman of some distinction. Perhaps she would have been happier if circumstances had allowed her some 'worldly' occasions for making the most of herself. But there were no such opportunities; nor were the Rowntrees much interested in the things towards which her own tastes inclined. She was musical, and she liked to paint in water-colour; and they had, on the whole, very little interest in the arts.

There were business difficulties in plenty during Joseph's first years at Tanner's Moat, and his domestic life was not, perhaps, altogether without irritation. But in the wider world he had the exciting satisfaction of seeing many of his hopes turn into facts. The early seventies were the most active period for social legislation of the whole century. Between 1870 and 1876 the 'reformed' Parliament passed, among others, two Education Acts, a Factory Act, a Secret Ballot Act, a Public Health Act, a Mines Act, and a Merchant Shipping Act; all of them measures whose importance was not lost upon Joseph. He followed the debates closely, and in 1870 he wrote to George Leeman, who was the Liberal member for York, about the first Education Bill which was having a fierce passage through the House of Commons.

Mr Leeman replied: 'I will be at my post on Monday night . . . I don't anticipate any explosion in the Lords about a ballot [for the selection of school boards] but the bill is so bad that I should not care much if the Lords *were* to turn stupid. We should get a better bill another day.'

Poor Mr Leeman must have had a hard time of it on that hot Monday night in July. There were fourteen divisions over the Government's proposal that school boards should be chosen by secret ballot, and it was five o'clock in the morning before the opposition 'saw reason', and the exhausted politicians went home by daylight.

The member for York was not alone in his opinion of the Education Bill. John Bright said it was the worst Act passed by any Liberal Parliament since 1832. Gladstone was far from happy about it. Yet, in the circumstances, perhaps it was humanly impossible to have produced anything better. Everyone agreed that children should be educated. No one would commit themselves to the pronouncement that education could be purely secular. But in a nation which possessed a State Church, a not inconsiderable Roman Catholic population, and several different Nonconformist bodies, who was to decide what form religious education should take? And, even more important, who was to pay for it?

This, finally, was the root of all the bitter arguments. If a school was subsidized by a comprehensive local rate levied upon householders whose religious allegiance might lie anywhere between the Pope and George Fox, it was going to be impossible to instruct all their offspring in the creeds, or lack of creeds, to which they had been accustomed. On the other hand, no one agreed to the Parliamentary proposal that the 'teaching of scriptures in rate schools should not be in favour of, or opposed to, the tenets of *any* denomination'. There were some practical men in Parliament in those days, and probably they saw exactly where such a proposal would lead.

Finally the Bill passed, with a large financial grant in favour of the Church of England schools and much discontent among the Nonconformists. What Joseph thought about it is not recorded, but he may well have felt, as did many other realists from Queen Victoria to John Bright, that the great thing was to get the children into school at almost any cost.

In some ways Joseph remained a student all his life. He had contracted the habit of reading very early and he never lost it. Tanner's Moat, politics, committees, or family life—none of them managed to stop him devouring the printed word. Moreover, he remembered what he read. One of his sons remarked that this was no wonder—he talked about what he was reading to everyone who came to the house.

Joseph's relationship with his children was as free and unstrained as his parents' had been with him. In his household, as in the Pavement one, there were few rules and a general assumption that the children were rational beings who would respond to reasonable treatment. On the whole the assumption was justified, though John Wilhelm, the eldest, had in youth a very violent temper. He once bit a woman friend of his mother's so severely that she bore the scar for years—an odd sidelight on the early history of the man who was later to become so outstanding a figure in the spiritual life of the Society of Friends.

Two more sons were born to Joseph and Antoinette in these years, Joseph Stephenson, known as Stephen, in 1875, and Oscar in 1879. Antoinette was now too tied by her domestic responsibilities to go about a great deal with her husband; but as his outings were generally connected with Friends' Committees or Adult School business she probably did not mind very much. She had also begun to take a great interest in her health. She had neuralgia. She had a 'phantom pregnancy'. And here at last she found something in common with the family into which she had married, who, like many of their contemporaries, were deeply interested in illness. Their letters are full of their own symptoms, their relations' symptoms, and the usually inferior symptoms of their friends. 'A distinct threatening of hay-cold.' 'Very Harassing Cough.' 'Try not to get overdone.' Phrases like these occur in all their letters. The *best* that was ever said was that so-and-so was 'much in her usual fashion'.

Only Joseph, though his mother worried about his 'looks' very often, seems to have taken little interest in his health. It was usually good, and he had other things to think about.

At Tanner's Moat, things were still moving slowly. Rock Cocoa continued to be the mainstay of the business, but the firm also manufactured Iceland Moss Cocoa, Chocolate Powder, Hexagon Cocoa, Pearl Cocoa, Flake Cocoa, Farinaceous Cocoa, Chocolate Creams, Shilling Chocolate, Confectionery Chocolate, Shield Chocolate, Chocolate Drops, and halfpenny and penny Balls. There were odd side-lines, too. One was a granular effervescent citrate of magnesia, a sort of early fruit salts, and another was the local agency for the sale of Neave's Farinaceous Food for Infants. H. I. Rowntree & Co., in fact, were willing at this time to make or to sell almost any respectable foodstuff which might win them a small profit.

But somehow nothing was outstandingly successful. Perhaps the fact that the firm would not advertise its wares may have had something to do with its slow start. Joseph was opposed to advertisements of any kind; and the only publicity, in those early days, was supplied by dignified letters to wholesale customers.

4 The 'Elect' cocoa motor-
car, about 1897

aking goods to the station from Tanner's Moat factory
]

5 View of Haxby Road works (from a drawing)

Aerial view of Rowntrees' factory in 1956

He could also be quite uncompromisingly rude about anything which savoured of an unsubstantiated claim about the qualities of any of his firm's products.

There was a system at this time of selling cocoa to shops to be retailed under the shop's own name. Rowntree & Co. supplied the 'own name' labels for this sort of customer, and sent them out when they delivered the cocoa. Thus Brown's, who were grocers at Malton, and Smith's who were grocers at Pickering, would have their own labels: 'Brown's Homœopathic Cocoa', or 'Smith's Pure Rock Cocoa'. (The cocoa being, of course, made by Rowntree & Co.) An early letter written by Joseph condemns in no uncertain terms one shop who bought their 'own name' cocoa from Rowntree's.

'About Blank's Homœopathic Label. I extremely dislike the wording of this label and will be no party to supplying a new man with a similar one. It is *not* a pure ground cocoa. It is *not* produced from the finest Trinidad Nuts. It is *not* the "best for family use". In fact the whole thing is a sham, not very creditable to anyone concerned with it.'

Joseph and Henry Isaac trusted in the quality of the goods they sold to make their own impression upon the public. Their father had built up his grocery business on the theory that a well-stocked shop was more important than goods in the shop window. Indeed, in 1833 he had discontinued even the custom of giving his clients a present at Christmas—a practice designed to attract trade in the pre-advertising age. This break with tradition had, at the time, practically emptied his shop for a few weeks at the busiest season of the year. But in the long run it had been advantageous. His customers came back, and the next year his Christmas turn-over was as large as it had ever been. His sons conducted the business of Tanner's Moat on much the same principles. They knew their cocoa was good, and they thought that it would sell on its merits.

But advertising in the seventies, although it was not done on anything like the modern scale, had begun to be a factor in commercial success. Joseph and Henry Isaac put themselves at a considerable disadvantage by their policy.

They were handicapped, also, by the small scale of their operations. There was nothing like a 'melangeur' department (the technical term for a department where chocolate is produced and mixed) and all the chocolate, according to one old employee's account, was made by a staff of seven men. They took turns in 'grinding, roasting, rubbing, and fetching in the sugar'. Two small machines did the 'melanging' and eight hundredweight of chocolate was a very good day's work.

The chocolate-cream department was started by Hanks, the foreman already mentioned, with one girl as his assistant. Hanks seems to have been a very important person. As well as everything else he acted as night-watchman, for he lived next door to the factory. He also fetched the money on Saturdays for wages. Joseph and Henry Isaac paid the usual sort of wages for the time. Girls of fourteen started at about three shillings a week and boys at four. A man who earned eighteen shillings was doing well.

It would be difficult to make a true comparison between these wages and those of today, but as at this time men on the land earned between eight and fourteen shillings a week according to the locality, and a boy starting on a farm usually got fivepence a day, it may be deduced that the pay packets in the Rowntree factory were neither better nor worse than in other places. The hours were those commonly worked in well-organized factories: six to six except on Saturday, when everyone stopped at 2 p.m. There was a dinner-break of an hour, and two other short intervals, one in the morning and one in the afternoon. Cocoa was taken round for the men to drink in the mid-morning break.

The office staff—there were *two* clerks and *two* desks by 1875— did not have to appear until eight in the morning, but they frequently worked overtime at night. This seems to have been usual in many firms at this period, probably because some office work could not be finished off until the results of the day's work in the factory were known.

There is no doubt that in these years money was tight. Joseph's personal account books show how carefully he analysed and arranged his own income. He had bought a saddle horse in 1867 and a 'second-hand wagonette' in 1874. But at the end of that year he sold the horse and stored the wagonette. Although the horse saved him some train fares, since he used it for local business journeys, it cost him, on an average, twelve shillings and sevenpence-three-farthings a week, including food, shoeing medicine, and tolls on the road. It was not really an economic proposition.

In 1872, while his wife and his four-year-old son were at Hamburg with her father, Joseph travelled about northern Germany for three weeks with Benjamin Seebohm. The next summer he had a fortnight alone in Switzerland. But after that, for four years, he did not go abroad. Even by *not* keeping a horse he could not afford the foreign holidays he enjoyed so much. The business at Tanner's Moat, in spite of increased sales, had shown a loss of five hundred pounds in 1873.

CHAPTER NINE

THERE may be no connection between two journeys which Joseph made to Birmingham in 1875 and two very short visits he paid to Holland early in 1877, but it seems possible that he was exploring a new method of making cocoa. The Cadbury brothers, in their Birmingham factory, had installed a Dutch machine which extracted the fat from the cocoa beans by hydraulic pressure. What remained was cocoa as it is known today, a very light powder which could be sold unblended with sugar or anything else. Probably Joseph made enquiries about this process, for his journeys to Holland are set down in his account book as 'business expenses'. He also records that he spent his holiday that year in Switzerland 'with the Cadbury's', which indicates a closer relationship with that family than is noticeable at any other period.

But nothing came of Joseph's investigations for a long time. Perhaps he felt that the cost of the Dutch machines was too high to be justifiable, even though the business at Tanner's Moat was now showing a small profit. It would be more prudent to try an experiment which demanded no more initial outlay than a boiling-pan and the services of one man and a boy.

It was in 1879 that a Frenchman named Claude Gaget called upon Joseph and Henry Isaac with a sample of some gums which he had made. The manufacture of gums and pastilles was at this time almost a monopoly of the French. No firm in England had yet produced anything to compare with those which were imported, and Joseph and Henry Isaac decided to try their hand.

'Crystallized Gum Pastilles' were put on sale by Rowntrees early in 1881, and it quickly became apparent that they were a great success. They were sold loose in four-pound wooden boxes and retailed at a penny an ounce. Claude Gaget's one boy and one boiling-pot were soon found inadequate to deal with the increasing orders, and there is reason to believe that it was largely because of the Gums that Rowntrees were employing twice as many people in 1883 as they had done in 1880.

This hopeful state of affairs is joyfully, though modestly, reflected in Joseph's personal expenditure. In 1881 he went abroad *twice*; in June with his wife and children to Germany, and in August to Switzerland with friends.

All over England, in the early eighties, trade was good and industrial output was increasing. But the Rowntree brothers were still in a dangerous position. They were employing two hundred people, but their margin of profit was not large. And in 1883 there began to be threatening signs of another trade depression.

This was a bad year for the whole family. Joseph's nephew, the eldest son of his brother John, died in the autumn; and so did his sister Hannah's two young daughters, who had caught typhoid fever while on holiday in the country. But the death which affected Joseph most was that of Henry Isaac in May.

He was ill only for a few days, and his death certificate gives the cause of death as peritonitis. It is said—and it seems likely—that he had a sudden attack of acute appendicitis, for which there was then no surgical remedy.

Henry Isaac was forty-five when he died, and he left a widow and three children—the eldest a boy of fifteen. He also left Joseph alone in the factory which they had managed together.

The death of Henry Isaac meant more to Joseph, however, than the loss of a brother and partner. Henry Isaac had been witty, gay and light-hearted—three characteristics which were not common in the Rowntree family. He had a sense of fun and a delicate unmalicious irony which made a joke out of small setbacks and caused larger decisions to appear less anxiously portentous. After he died there was no one at Tanner's Moat who could make Joseph laugh in a grim moment, or turn some commercial reverse into a jest.

There were some extremely grim moments indeed after Henry Isaac's death. It was Joseph's bad luck to be left alone just at a time when trade began to be difficult again, and when prices were falling all over the country. The accounts for the first half of the year 1883 show that the Firm made a loss of £385.

He must have wondered whether he would be able to carry on the business at all. The Firm had just bought some land at Foss Islands, which was never in fact used, and also a flour mill in North Street adjoining Tanner's Moat, because they urgently needed more space for the manufacture of the Crystallized Gums. Money had had to be raised for the purchases, and when his brother died Joseph's own capital only amounted to £8,000 out of the Firm's total of £29,000. There was another £7,500 which had been lent by various relations; but over £12,000 remained in the form of mortgages and bank overdrafts. The interest was a heavy drain on the small factory struggling to keep working through a general slump.

Those years from 1883 to 1886 became increasingly difficult in most industries. Shipbuilding yards were turning out only half as much tonnage at the end of them as they had done at the beginning. Cotton and iron production fell considerably; and things were so bad by 1886 that a Royal Commission was appointed to enquire into the Depression of Trade.

But somehow Joseph surmounted his difficulties, and even continued the annual holidays abroad which were his only real luxury. In the August after Henry Isaac's death he took his wife and the three elder children to Switzerland for the first time, and the next year he and John Wilhelm, who was then nearly sixteen, had a month together at Mürren. This latter journey established a tradition. One by one, as they grew up, Joseph took each of his children for a holiday alone with him abroad. Anyone brought up in a large family will know the particular pleasure of being thus singled out of the crowd for an uninterrupted month with a congenial parent; and between John Wilhelm and Joseph there was already a bond of shared interests as well as affection.

In spite of the claims of Tanner's Moat, Joseph had always found time to enjoy his children. His family life followed a pattern not very different from that of his own youth. His children did their lessons with a governess, and he kept an eye on their curriculum and encouraged their hobbies. At his dinner-table, as at his father's, the conversation was of books and politics, of the doings of Friends and the problems of relations. Fashions, sport, painting, music, or the theatre were seldom mentioned and certainly not discussed. They were all outside Joseph's range of interest. Antoinette still played the piano and encouraged the children to paint; but most of them were not much interested in the arts.

John Wilhelm, however, showed some talent for painting, and in later years he made a break with family tradition by becoming passionately interested in the theatre. He was, himself, a singularly gifted amateur actor.

The Rowntrees had moved again in 1882, and were now living in a house at the bottom of St. Mary's, the street which turned off Bootham and led towards the river. The establishment seems to have been too small for them, since they rented a piece of garden from a neighbour, and also a 'schoolroom' in Joseph's mother's house at the top of the road. When Joseph's youngest child, a daughter called Winifred, was born in 1884, yet another move was made; this time to a house next door to Sarah Rowntree.

The rents of these houses did not vary very much; the first one belonging to Bootham School had cost Joseph seventy pounds a year, the last one next door to his mother's cost him seventy-seven. They were staffed, as time went on, by four maids and an odd-job man, instead of the two maids and a German nursery-governess of earlier years, but Joseph's bill for domestic service was not high. In 1868 the total had been forty-five pounds a year, in 1885 it was eighty-nine. This latter sum covered the wages not only of four maids and a man, but also included the new baby's nurse, who was paid twenty pounds a year. The governess's salary was a separate item. It was ten pounds a quarter, which was high pay for the time, but she had to teach three boys and a girl until they were about twelve.

Joseph's three elder sons went straight from the family schoolroom to Bootham School as he himself had done; but the youngest boy, Oscar, was sent to a day-school when he was only eight. There was a gap of four years between Oscar and his next brother, and perhaps Joseph thought it extravagant to keep a governess to teach one child. But it was a break with tradition, and it was not the only one. The elder daughter, Agnes, was sent to York High School for nearly five years before she went to the Quaker school called The Mount. The old pattern was beginning to change.

To have sons is sometimes a commercial asset. If they are young men of personality they may become a valuable liaison between the owner of a firm and his employees. Things may be hinted to a boy of seventeen which it would be hard to say even to the most enlightened proprietor of a business; and, equally, a son may contradict his father more boldly than most employees would venture to do.

Joseph's children had not been brought up on the theory that 'Father knows best'. When the boys went to work at Tanner's Moat they saw no reason why they should not make critical suggestions about the running of the business. If Joseph had any temptation to sink into a comfortable conventional rut it was removed once and for all by John Wilhelm and Seebohm.

John Wilhelm was seventeen and had just left school when he started to work in the factory. It was 1885, Henry Isaac had been dead for two years, and the firm was employing two hundred people. John Wilhelm and Seebohm—who went to Tanner's Moat three years after his brother—were not formally apprenticed to their father, but they were sent to every department of the factory in turn to become 'thoroughly acquainted with the *practical* side of the work'. Joseph had served his time as an apprentice in the Pavement shop, on the same terms as the other boys. He knew the value of that experience, and in the case of his own children he repeated the essential pattern, though the details were a little different. His sons did not learn to manage machinery as Joseph had once learned to handle the coffee-roaster, but they stayed long enough in each workroom to understand all the various processes. And before he was nineteen John Wilhelm had begun to reorganize the cocoa and chocolate departments.

Perhaps because they were 'put through the mill' in this way both boys achieved a good relationship with the other employees. Their presence was not resented because they were the owner's sons, nor do they seem to have been regarded with suspicion. Nevertheless, for John Wilhelm, it cannot have been an easy life. He was a delicate boy who had begun to go deaf as a child. An ear-trumpet had to be bought for him when he was only nine, and in his last year at school he had to sit close to the master who was teaching in order to follow the lesson. But he was quick and observant, and the men at Tanner's Moat found him congenial. He was learning to restrain the temper which had once been so violent, and he was less 'quizzical' than he had been in his schooldays. The people with whom he worked found him courageous and kindly, and came to value his jokes. There was a keen edge to his wit which could enliven the dullest workroom.

The factory was making progress now, but in many ways it was still in the stage of improvisation. More space was constantly needed. The flour mill in North Street had been altered, and several additional storeys of workrooms had been built above Joseph's office, but the equipment of the place was not lavish. There were only two coke-fired roasters for the cocoa beans, and there was no mechanical method of getting them on and off the fires. There was one joiner, who worked in a little room measuring eight feet by six, and the engineering department, according to one account, consisted of one man, a hand hammer, a cold chisel, and a file or two.

Nevertheless there were a hundred different 'lines' on sale, Gaget's boiling-pans were turning out four tons of gums and pastilles a week, and by 1887 a flat horse-drawn lorry was needed *every* day to take the factory's output to the station.

These were years when trade was good again in England, and Joseph took advantage of it. Every year he bought new property or added on to the old. Six cottages and a stable nearby in Queen Street were pulled down to make a three-storey building. More rooms were added to the old flour mill. Finally, in 1888, some small houses next to the office were bought in and replaced by six storeys of workrooms.

These piecemeal additions were far from satisfactory. There were no lifts, even in the six-storey building, and there are men still living who remember painfully the flights of stairs they used to climb in their early working days. Refrigeration was difficult, and in hot weather orders accumulated considerably. Seebohm, in his old age, said with some emphasis that 'Tanner's Moat was Hell'. It was not a word he used lightly.

Nevertheless, in spite of everything, the business was really making money at last.

The fact that Joseph had now changed his mind about advertising no doubt helped towards the expansion of the Firm's trade. There is no record of Rowntrees' first advertisement, and no explanation of Joseph's change of policy. It is possible that John Wilhelm influenced his father, for he was an extremely up-to-date young man and applied his considerable intelligence to every aspect of the business. Certainly advertising was started about two years after he began to work in the factory.

The early advertisements were of a sober description, but perhaps they were no less effective on that account. Dignity was still admired in the eighties, and a plain statement has a way of carrying its own conviction. *Tit-Bits* and *Answers* were the papers in which Rowntrees' original advertisements appeared, and one-eighth of a page cost £35. This was considered alarmingly high, but the expense soon proved justifiable.

It was possible, now, for Joseph to think again about the new method of making cocoa which his finances had made impracticable in earlier years. He engaged a Dutchman called Cornelius Hollander, and installed him in rooms at the top of the old flour mill. To safeguard the secrets of his process an iron door and a padlock were fitted to the entrance of his department, but these mysterious precautions did not last very long. 'Elect' cocoa was soon being manufactured in ordinary workrooms, and an Englishman called Archer, who had been the Firm's first engineer, succeeded Hollander as the person responsible for it.

The new process quickly proved its worth. 'Elect' began to compete almost at once with the older forms of cocoa. It was the modern product, a powder from which the surplus fat had been extracted, and there was no need to add sugar or arrowroot before putting it on sale. The name emphasized its undiluted purity, for elect was an adjective used in the druggists' trade to describe quality. It is said to have been suggested to Joseph by a manufacturing chemist.

'Elect' cocoa was first put on the market in 1887, a year in which prices were rising; and, like the Gums in 1881, it had a good start. If these two mainstays of the business had first appeared at a less propitious moment the story might have been different. The period from 1875 to 1886 is sometimes called 'the great depression', but there were several marked fluctuations in trade in those eleven years. Joseph's most important ventures were both launched on a tide of comparative prosperity. Was this good luck or good judgement on his part? Or, perhaps, a mixture of the two?

CHAPTER TEN

IT was not yet the age of technical experts, and the versatility of the men who worked at Tanner's Moat bears witness to their adaptability. A man who was engaged as a timekeeper in 1885 moved on to 'general oversight' of the factory a few years later. He was John Wilhelm's assistant in this case. Soon afterwards he became entirely responsible for the 'melangeur' and 'cake-room' departments (the latter being the place where cake or block chocolate was made) and for some time he also engaged the factory staff. Another man who had been a junior clerk in the office in 1879 later switched to the 'cream' rooms, where centres were made for cream chocolates, and presently found himself in charge of twenty people. Before he retired his department employed a thousand. Archer, the engineer who had been engaged in 1882, and who later became responsible for 'Elect' cocoa, eventually had a department of similar size.

Men of this type were Joseph's mainstay. They knew the factory as a whole. They had watched it grow. They understood the relationship between the different departments, and they could make allowances for makeshift workrooms and awkward equipment. In a sense they were amateurs, but they had a comprehensive idea of the business which was worth, at this period, much more than specialized training. They were an important part of the picture during the years when the business quadrupled the number of its employees. This actually happened between 1883, when Henry Isaac died, and 1894; in those eleven years the number of people employed at Rowntrees rose from two hundred to eight hundred and ninety-four.

The size of his staff began to worry Joseph long before it reached the eight-hundred mark. There came a moment when he no longer knew all his employees as his father had known the Pavement 'family' of apprentices, or as he himself had known his first workers at Tanner's Moat. It is impossible to know hundreds of people at all intimately—impossible to see whether they are ill or well, happy or unhappy, doing good work or bad. Joseph could delegate responsibility more thoroughly than most men, but the welfare of a firm's work-people was something which he had been brought up to believe was the proper responsibility of the owner and of the owner alone. Moreover, he had a horror of the 'laissez-faire' attitude towards labour. It was the unhappy legacy of the Industrial Revolution, and of the rugged economic policy which marked the nineteenth-century's middle decades. Even in the nineties it could still be said that for many manufacturers 'Labour was just a factor in production, a commodity to be bought and sold in accordance with the higgling of the market. That it was housed in a human body and impelled by a human soul were no more than accidental factors which had no bearing on its usefulness'.[1]

Such an attitude could only be abhorrent to a man like Joseph, to whom individuals were always persons first and employees afterwards. But it was difficult to see how, in the changed conditions at Tanner's Moat, his old ideals were to survive.

Joseph had known the paternal system at its best, and he may have seen its passing with reluctance. But he must have been aware, too, of its dangers. Its success depended on the character of the 'master', and however intimately an employer knew his men, however friendly his relationship with them, there was nothing to stop him 'compelling them to work in unwholesome conditions, to put in destructively long hours, to forgo many of the benefits of civilized life, to fight for every penny of every wage increase, and to become paupers when his own negligence or parsimony left them the victims of an unguarded machine'.[2]

Benevolent autocracy had worked very well in the Pavement shop, but Joseph was much too realistic to believe that the majority of employers were as intelligent and imaginative as his father. Also, when it came to large-scale undertakings, even intelligence and high principles were not sufficient safeguards. They could vanish overnight, through death or illness or a

[1] Urwick & Brech. *The Making of Scientific Management.*   [2] ibid.

change in management, and leave a thousand employees at the mercy of quite a different kind of master. It was essential to work out a less precarious system of industrial government, and one permanent enough to survive the changes and chances of a single man's life. But the responsibility for this development still lay with those at the head of their firms. The workers could claim their rights under the Factory and Workshop Acts, and they could strike if they did not get them, but it was not in *their* power to introduce the sort of constructive policy which could cement a business together and make a whole out of all its parts. This was the challenge which faced the men in authority, even though most of them did not yet realize it.

Joseph understood the problem and wrestled with it in the abstract, but for a long time he remained autocratic in practice. He made his own decisions and gave his employees such things as he thought it good for them to have. One of these was a library.

It was started about 1885, when the firm was not yet in a position to spend money on unnecessary frills. Joseph provided ten pounds out of his own purse, and another ten pounds was given as a grant by the 'Pure Literature Society'. Books described as mainly suitable for young people were then bought, and one penny a week was arbitrarily deducted from the wages of every single employee for the upkeep of the library. There is no record of anyone objecting to this, in spite of the fact that they had not been consulted about a reduction in pay which amounted to two per cent in a large number of cases. People were still accustomed to having things done to them 'for their own good'.

In the world of late nineteenth-century industry even such authoritative benevolence was not very usual. There was a general feeling among employers that legislation had now done all that was necessary for the workers—and sometimes more. Women and children had their hours of labour controlled, which was often *very* inconvenient for the firm employing them, and safety and sanitary conditions had been imposed on all the more dangerous trades in 1875. Most of the men who owned or managed factories felt quite convinced that if they kept to the regulations they were doing all that could be expected of them.

This was the attitude which Joseph challenged, and thereby joined a small and honourable company of business men who managed their firms in an unfashionable way.

Such magnates were few and far between, but a few stand out among all the horrors of industry's dark age. Some were Quakers, as Carlyle noticed. 'Friend Prudence keeps a thousand workmen; has striven in all ways to attach them to him; has provided conversational soirees, playgrounds, bands of music for the young. ... A certain person called Blank, living over the way, also keeps about a thousand men. He has done nothing but pay wages according to supply-and-demand. Blank's workers are perpetually in mutiny; every six months he has a strike, every day and every hour they are fretting and obstructing, pilfering, wasting and idling. "I would not", says Friend Prudence, "exchange my workers for his *with seven thousand pounds to boot*".'[1]

There were others besides Friends who contrived, even in the years when the cheapness of labour was the only general consideration, to run their businesses both successfully and humanely. But almost without exception these strangely unorthodox employers came from families who, like the Quakers, had for one reason or another remained a little aloof from their surroundings. Sometimes they were of foreign extraction, like the Courtaulds; sometimes, like the Wedgwoods, they simply chose to be 'different'. They lived, in spirit if not in fact, 'over the shop'. They might have country estates but they would not mix much with the aristocracy. Their daughters were not presented at Court. Their sons were allowed to hunt only because intolerance of other people's pleasures was intolerable. They made large fortunes and gave large slices of them away. They knew their workpeople and fought for their interests. Much of the legislation to safeguard those who worked in dangerous trades was urged upon Parliament by employers like the Wedgwoods, who saw each generation of potters growing 'more stunted and weaker than the last'.

It was men of this type, not swayed by other people's opinions, not socially ambitious, not afraid to be thought eccentric, and

[1] Carlyle. *Past and Present*, Book IV.

confident of their own power to go on making money, who laid the foundations of a new order in industry. But there were very few of these pioneers and progress was slow.

The Courtauld silk-weavers in Essex once collected their pennies and gave a great dinner to their employers as a token of appreciation for 'the care and kind consideration' with which they had always been treated. They made all the arrangements themselves. 'The idea spread from room to room and from factory to factory like wildfire.' They put up a great marquee in the meadow outside Mr Samuel Courtauld's house, and the party, which was called a Factory Festival, was attended by every man, woman, and child in the firm. Six oxen were roasted, there were gallons of beer and cider, hundreds of pies and cakes, and, later, jugs of tea. 'There was gaiety without disorder, gratitude without servility, and independence without rudeness,' said the reporter from the Halstead newspaper. There were, also, many speeches. Mr Courtauld referred to 'the era which has now dawned upon the sons of toil, when the buyers and sellers of labour can regard each other as friends whose interests are the same'.

The date was 1846. Mr Courtauld could not know that in many parts of the industrial world his new era would still not have dawned a hundred years later.

The pattern changed gradually. 'Care and kind consideration' in progressive firms began to develop into 'welfare' in the technical modern sense of the word. But it was not, even by the most advanced employers, regarded as an integral part of factory management until the nineteenth century was over. A public-spirited man, in the eighties, might devote time and money to the extramural care of his employees, but there was a general belief that the evils of industrial employment were inevitable. 'A factory might, indeed must, be a slum—human nature being human nature and competition being competition—but the misfortunes of those condemned to such accommodation should be palliated by some district-visiting.'[1]

Joseph Rowntree never had much use for palliatives, and he

[1] Urwick & Brech. *The Making of Scientific Management.*

had already decided to move his business away from Tanner's Moat before he engaged his first 'welfare worker'. He had every intention of changing the unprepossessing character of his work-rooms, but the change would take time. And in the meanwhile someone must be found to look after the ever-increasing numbers of girls who now worked at Rowntrees.

These children of thirteen and fourteen, who came to the factory as soon as they left school, found themselves in a man-made world. The half-dozen departments between which the work was now divided all had men at the head of them. There were no women in positions of authority, and a foreman ruled in every workroom.

Joseph, as yet, saw no reason to change this practice, which was the usual one in factories. Probably, even if he had wished to replace foremen by forewomen it would have been impossible to do so, because the majority of girls left to get married by the time they were about twenty. Women of sufficient age and character to undertake responsibility would have been hard to find. Yet, as more and more girls came to Tanner's Moat, it began to seem unsuitable that there should be no grown-up woman to whom they could turn when in difficulty, and no female authority to advise the men for whom they worked. It was to fill this need that in 1891 Joseph appointed a lady 'to take charge of the girl staff's health, behaviour, etc.'.

Such an appointment was revolutionary, though as long ago as 1864 a Factory Inspector's report had urged that wherever large numbers of women were employed a 'married female of mature age' ought to be engaged as an 'onlooker'. The report had added that the owner of a business would find such an appointment greatly to his own advantage; but not many business men had been able to believe this. The first welfare-worker at Rowntrees held the position of a pioneer.

It is quite likely that she was not immediately welcomed by her young charges. She was strict about some things which no man would have noticed. She set her face against embroidery trimmings and coloured frocks, and ordained that the girls must all come to work in black dresses. Blouses and skirts were forbidden after one child appeared in a blouse whose collar failed to cover her throat.

'This', said the welfare worker, 'might easily draw a man's attention to you.'

But if there was any resentment felt in the factory about the new appointment it must have been short-lived, for in a year's time an assistant welfare-worker was engaged. The first lady by then had proved her worth, and so many little odd jobs had been handed over to her that she had no time to deal with them all alone. It was she who now ran the lending library, and took pains to see that people were supplied with the kind of book they might really like to read. She dealt with girls who fell ill, investigated absentees, helped to arrange social festivities, and was at the beck and call of everyone with a decision to make or a problem to solve. The management found her very useful, and in spite of the new rules which she imposed upon the girls they accepted her authority. Her prim regulations about dress and behaviour were counterbalanced by a genuine kindliness towards her charges.

Joseph was feeling his way into a new world in these later years at Tanner's Moat, and inevitably some of his projects were unsuccessful. One of these was the Cocoa Works Debating Society, inspired by a similar institution which Joseph and his brother John had once formed among the apprentices and journeymen of the grocery shop. The Pavement Debating Society had been popular, but the one at Tanner's Moat was not. Joseph attended it himself, and some of the discussions are said to have reached a high intellectual level. Nevertheless the younger employees were not interested and the older ones were too busy to keep it going for long. It was quietly abandoned some time in 1885.

Another and more spectacular failure was an outing for which a special train was engaged to take all the Firm's work-people to spend a day by the sea. The plan was that those who wished to do so should leave the train at Goathland, walk over the moors to Whitby, and there rejoin the others for a pleasant afternoon on the beach. Unfortunately the day was wet, and the moorland party was soaked to the skin by the time they reached Whitby. The public-houses were warm and welcoming, and while their clothes steamed by the fire Rowntrees' workers took more refreshment than was perhaps usual for them. Some, by the end of the day, were quite unmistakeably drunk, and the police had to escort them to the train.

Joseph must have been a good deal shaken by such an ending to the expedition he had planned; and certainly, for a good many years, there were no more outings.

Nevertheless he continued his experiments. Calmly and persistently he tried to keep pace with the changing conditions of his business; to bridge the gap not only between employers and employed but also between the different groups of people in the factory itself. He arranged occasional festivities to include the whole Firm, such as the so-called 'concerts' in the Exhibition Buildings near Bootham. Tables were laid with a substantial meal, and there were recitations as well as music. Such gatherings were very popular, for there were few entertainments of any sort in the nineties which working people could afford.

The office staff, who were still not very numerous, were often invited to 'social evenings' at Joseph's own house. He had a close personal connection with these boys and men, and he interviewed all new applicants for an office job himself. Such interviews are bound to be awe-inspiring, but there are men who can still remember Joseph's skill in putting them at their ease when they were shy boys of thirteen.

Office work in the eighties became quite separate from the manufacturing side of Tanner's Moat. No longer were the office staff required to take off their coats and help to move sacks of sugar or cocoa. But they worked very hard. There was no time nowadays to read all the postcards and make guesses about the letters before Joseph came to inspect the post-bag. In the evenings it was often after nine o'clock when they left the Works, and it was the job of the youngest office-boy to cross Lendal Bridge with the letters for the ten o'clock post. To keep themselves going the office staff sometimes bought sandwiches from a hotel around the corner; beautiful sandwiches with a thick slice

of York ham and real butter on the good new bread. But the
sandwiches cost threepence for two rounds, and overtime was
only paid at the rate of a penny-halfpenny an hour, so they were
considered by many to be an unjustifiable extravagance.

Joseph, oddly enough, does not seem to have noticed that his
office staff was overworked. But his attention was abruptly
drawn to the fact when a young clerk asked if he might leave at
6 p.m. on one evening in every week because he needed the time
for private study.

'Surely', Joseph said, 'one evening is not enough?'

The boy admitted that it was not; but he added that even one
evening to himself would be a godsend. This frank statement led
in due course to a good deal of reorganization in the office.
Extra staff were engaged and working hours became shorter;
though still, in the busy season, some men had to do overtime.
There were no 'enumerators' in those days, and all numbers had
to be written in after the factory work was over.

Still the office seems to have been a congenial place on the
whole. There were no women workers in offices then or for
many years thereafter, and the boys in their teens made up a
cheerful company. They were under the control of a head clerk;
a man who was fussy about issuing new pen-nibs, but who
nevertheless always came back from lunch stamping his feet
loudly and whistling 'Now the day is over' to warn his under-
lings of his approach. There were office jokes and office traditions; and letters still dropped from the owner's office through a
trap-door in the ceiling together with an occasional request for
penny buns.

The commercial travellers, too, provided mild excitement as
they came and went to their interviews with Joseph. There were
now half a dozen of these gentlemen, and they were very grand
indeed. They wore tall silk hats and frock-coats and were unmistakably Personages; and for some reason those who represented the Firm in Scotland were always the most imposing.

After 1886 Joseph's business never encountered any serious
setbacks. He had sold £55,000 worth of goods in 1883, and seven

years later his sales were more than double that amount. But the anxious earlier years were still too near to be forgotten. He kept, as he had always done, a scrupulous account of his own expenses, and his children were required to do the same. He gave them, however, rather generous allowances—John Wilhelm had thirty pounds a year when he was nineteen—which was regarded as pocket money and could be spent without questions being asked or accounts expected.

It was 1890 before Joseph felt that he could again afford a horse, and he did not 'set up his carriage' properly until 1892. The first vehicle to replace the wagonette which had been given up fifteen years before was a modest 'governess trap' costing only nineteen pounds. Some of Joseph's friends thought that he could have afforded a carriage-and-pair long before he bought his first landau and two mares called Molly and Princess Sheila. But, like his father before him, he had no wish to find himself in a social category of whose other inhabitants he often disapproved. A carriage was a definite sign of a family's wealth and standing in the nineties, and the 'carriage trade' was a shopkeeper's description of his richer customers. Joseph postponed for as long as possible the moment when his equipage must inevitably proclaim his prosperity. Even after the landau was bought—it cost £130—he never used it unless he was going out with his wife.

Holidays abroad, on the other hand, Joseph took without misgiving. Generally he went to Switzerland for the month of August, taking one of his children or a friend with him, and once inviting the original welfare-worker from the factory as his guest. These journeys were not, in point of fact, unduly expensive. The average cost of four weeks in Switzerland, including a first-class return ticket from York, was only twenty-two pounds in the nineties. It was a modest sum when compared with the three hundred or so a year which Joseph was now spending on his children's education, or the equally large amounts which he set down annually under the heading 'subscriptions and charity'. These were big outgoings—they would perhaps have to be quadrupled to represent equivalent amounts today—but Joseph had no need to worry about them. His business was now prospering beyond all expectation.

Tanner's Moat, nevertheless, was flourishing under difficulties. Looking at the factory which had grown up bit by bit on the foundations of a disused iron-foundry, Joseph was aware of all its drawbacks. Many of the workrooms were dark and inconvenient. There were not nearly enough cloakrooms and lavatories. The time was long past when wet coats could be hung to dry in the roasting-room and hot drinks could be brewed for a handful of men working overtime. Girls who came to work through pouring rain nowadays had to put damp coats on again at the end of the day. There were no means of providing hot food for anyone, or even cups of tea.

An enterprising foreman from the Gum room once tried to run a fried-fish stall, and it was much appreciated for a time. But mischievous boys played tricks on him, luring him away and helping themselves to fish in his absence, and he gave it up in disgust.

After this the workers who came from a distance had no alternative except to eat sandwiches in a bare room too small to accommodate them all at the same time.

In Joseph's eyes Tanner's Moat had now none of the advantages either of the old world or the new. His long-ago half-domestic arrangements for his employees had been outgrown, and there was no space to try more scientific large-scale methods. The time had come to move.

As far as the actual work of the factory was concerned it could have remained where it was for at least several years more. There was still property for sale in some of the adjacent streets, and there was also the land at Foss Islands which Henry Isaac had bought and which had never yet been used. Joseph must have considered all this very carefully before he made his decision; but at last, in 1890, he bought twenty-nine acres of land in Haxby Road, on the outskirts of the city. He was going to build a new factory, large, light, and properly equipped for the work which it was meant to do. Furthermore, and perhaps for him this was truly the deciding factor, the new factory could be furnished with those amenities which might make it easier for men and women 'to develop all that is best and most worthy in themselves'.

Joseph's words have an old-fashioned ring. They must be translated by a phrase such as 'Industry's social obligation to the worker is to make his work as interesting and satisfying as possible',[1] if they are to convey any of his meaning to modern ears.

[1] V. M. Clarke. *New Times, New Methods, and New Men.* (George Allen & Unwin).

CHAPTER ELEVEN

TWO people died in 1888 who had been important to Joseph. One was John Bright, the hero of his boyhood. In his early twenties Joseph had stayed with Bright in his bare house at Rochdale, and had found there, probably for the first time, an opportunity to discuss politics with a man who knew them at first-hand. These visits had given the young man from Pavement exciting glimpses of a world far removed from the enclosed Quaker setting in which he normally lived. Later on Joseph came to disagree with Bright over Home Rule for Ireland; he upheld Gladstone's policy. But when Bright spoke on the Reform Bill, Free Trade, the Egyptian Campaign, and the necessity for curbing the power of the House of Lords, he said publicly many things with which Joseph's private judgement agreed. His voice was to echo in the younger man's ears for a long time after his death.

The other person who died in 1888 was Sarah Rowntree, Joseph's mother. She was eighty-two, but she 'got about the house' to the last, received innumerable callers, and did not lose interest in her children, her grand children, or the activities of Friends. With her death a very long link with the past was broken for her son. He could remember her, nearly fifty years before, reading to him in the drawing-room above the Pavement shop, and telling him how she had seen the first passenger train in the world, when she was a girl living at Stockton.

Sarah Rowntree, in her will, gave to her three surviving children the option to buy, for £2,600, the house which her husband had built and in which she lived until her death. It was Joseph who bought it, and he moved into it in the spring of 1888. It was still divided, as it had been originally for Julia and himself, and in the smaller part Henry Isaac's widow and her three children were established. They had been there for some time, and they did not move when Joseph and his wife took over Sarah's part of the house; though by now, perhaps, some of the connecting doors had been suppressed.

In the family the house now came to be known as 'Top House', because it stood at the top of St. Mary's. It was one of a number of Rowntree establishments in the neighbourhood. By the end of the nineties two of Joseph's sons and one of his nephews were married, and all three had set up house in St. Mary's. Geographically at least they kept very close together as a family.

Joseph was fifty-two when he moved into Top House. His hair was not yet grey, and he still wore a thick dark beard. Perhaps because he was energetic and quick-moving he had never put on weight, and his blue eyes were as bright as ever. He was gayer now than he had been as a young man. The face which had been 'serious and pensive' in his twenties now looked very often as though he had just thought of something amusing.

It was a good period in his life. His financial worries were over, and his children were growing up into the sort of people with whom he could discuss his real interests.

The fact that his sons were no traditionalists he found in itself a comfort. They took nothing at second-hand. They could be trusted to interpret, in their own idiom, such of his beliefs as they accepted. What they could not accept they would discard without apology. Joseph was pleased by this ruthlessness. He knew that the young must test and taste and throw away a great many things before they arrive at their own conclusions. And he knew that the process was not altogether pleasant.

He wrote once, to a girl at the Mount school: 'Don't insist that good things shall always come to you on a golden plate. Many a man robs himself of enriching influences by too great a fastidiousness, mental or moral. A vigorous nature will get its nourishment from almost any kind of food.'

Among Joseph's own children the one who had this 'vigorous nature' most strongly developed was John Wilhelm. His years in the factory had not blunted his naturally inquisitive mind, and his working life among men who were not Quakers, as well as his friendships with those who were, led him to criticize the Society of Friends publicly at the Yearly Meeting of 1893.

John Wilhelm had seriously thought of resigning his membership in the Society, and he spoke with feeling for the young and the doubtful. Much that was said in Meetings for Worship, he declared, entirely failed to reach his generation. He pleaded for religious messages 'in their own language', in the terms in which they spoke and thought themselves. And he condemned some of the Society's practices as 'Quaker caution and love of detail run to seed'.

This probably needed saying at this particular time, and John Wilhelm said it well. There was no trace of the prig about him. He was both gay and witty, though these qualities have been too little recorded. From chance contemporary tributes—'there was always some fun when he was about'—it is possible to deduce something of the essence of the man himself; though the usual pious compliments to his memory have done less than justice to this side of his nature. His serious writings remain and his fun and gaiety have been forgotten, so that the picture which comes down to later generations seems more stern than attractive.

The Society of Friends, on the whole, took John Wilhelm's criticism well. There were many 'Weighty Friends' who supported him, as in earlier times old men had spoken out against the crippling marriage regulations, and the 'plain dress and plain speech' which had been stumbling-blocks to the young people of their day. And certainly Joseph agreed with his son. He had watched him wrestling with doubts and intellectual difficulties; and had seen that in this era, when the new science challenged the old faith at every turn, any religious message, in Meeting or out of it, could only be repellent to the young if it blandly ignored all their problems.

Top House was a place still full of Quaker traditions, but every year saw some change from the habits of Friends in Joseph's own youth. John Wilhelm travelled abroad. Seebohm studied economics at Manchester. Stephen went as an undergraduate to Cambridge. They brought home friends who were not always Friends, and some ideas which would have startled the household in Pavement.

But Joseph himself, though he encouraged his children in these ventures, made few changes in his own habits. The elder Joseph would not have seen much difference in the house he had built forty years before. There was good food in it still, and good well-cared-for furniture; fine linen, many books, and few pictures. The garden was well cultivated but the hot-house fruit was almost invariably given away to invalids. (To eat it oneself bordered on *luxury*.) In the visitors' book three-quarters of the names were those of Friends.

It must have seemed, in some ways, a very curious household to Stephen's friends from Cambridge and Seebohm's from Manchester. It was a place with its own conventions. There was wealth combined with a deliberate lack of ostentation, a considerable amount of scholarship which owed nothing to any university, and a certain unconventionality which had nothing at all in common with Bohemia. Friends, in the nineties, still differed in many ways from the world of their time. The division was not rigidly marked, as it had been when Joseph was a boy, but the inner sense of separation remained. There were still many things which Quakers thought 'non-essential', and a great many more in which they were simply not interested.

The building of the new factory at Haxby Road began soon after the land was bought, but it was at Tanner's Moat, in the maze of small-windowed workrooms, among all the inconvenient makeshifts, that Joseph established the tradition which was to control the business of the future. It was not an easy thing to do, for now, bristling with complications, the two great problems of twentieth-century industry first appeared: the relationship between employers and employed, and the attitude of men and women to their work.

The old industrial life was disappearing. Joseph's business was no longer a little commercial unit where he and his workmen all knew each other and everything was on a personal basis; where laziness or inefficiency had immediate results, visible to everyone. In the beginning, at Tanner's Moat, men had worked hard and well, if only for the reason that the factory was their livelihood and its failure would have meant unemployment for them in a world where lack of work meant lack of food. On the lowest level they had a real interest in the Firm's prosperity. But for many of them there was more to it than this. They could take pride in their work, even if it was hard and monotonous, for they saw the results of it. They had an emotional stake in the factory which was often as real as the financial one.

Twenty-five years later the scene had changed entirely. Instead of an easily understood picture there was a panorama of different departments, and no one at the bottom of the Firm could have much comprehension of it as a whole. What was to replace that satisfaction in a man or woman's individual effort, which had gone so far to make work in the small factory tolerable in spite of long hours and difficult conditions?

Frustration has been described as the 'industrial disease' of modern times, and it is a fact that even good wages and comfortable surroundings are not always a cure for it. It is the begetter of irresponsible behaviour, it slows up production, and occasionally it produces strikes. It also causes much human unhappiness. But how is anyone to avoid feeling frustrated if his work is monotonous and he never sees its wider results? And if he has no true personal interest in the firm which employs him?

There were men at Tanner's Moat who had grown up with the Firm. Some could remember Henry Isaac in his shirt-sleeves helping to shift a new piece of machinery into position. Some had seen, with pride, two small 'melanging' machines replaced by a separate department which could produce a hundred times more chocolate. Some had worked at three or four different jobs, and been present at the birth of more than one new process. There was little chance of any of these men losing interest in a business which they had watched and helped through the difficult years of its establishment. But they were in a minority now. Year by year they were increasingly outnumbered by girls of thirteen and fourteen, who came to the Works straight from school. For these girls the long hours in the factory could hardly help being tedious. Their real life began at six in the evening, when they changed the unbecoming black dress which had usually been passed on by a mother or an aunt, and took out the heavy metal curlers which they often wore in their hair all day. Then, with well-frizzed heads and a bright frock, they could set about the business of living, even if it only meant running an errand to the shop on the corner and hoping to meet the boy from next door on the way.

Joseph realized the narrowness of the world in which his young employees existed. Even when their hours were shortened from fifty-four to forty-eight a week, it was still obvious that most of their waking life was spent inside Tanner's Moat. What was the factory giving them beyond their wages? Had they the satisfaction of learning a new skill, or making progress in a job they liked? Did they ever feel part of a group with a common purpose, or were they simply getting through boring hours as best they could?

These questions would become increasingly urgent as the business grew larger and larger, but they were not often raised at a time when most employers demanded only that an employee should be able to do a particular job efficiently; what the job might be doing to the man did not enter into their calculations.

Progressive owners, in the nineties, were improving the working conditions in their factories, but half a century was to go by before scientific investigation revealed that the fundamental needs of a human being went beyond good workshops, canteens, and playing fields. Joseph, who considered people and their requirements against a background of unchanging values and intangible necessities, made the discovery without difficulty.

Some of the 'amenities' of which Joseph had spoken appeared as soon as the new buildings at Haxby Road began to be used; but they were, in fact, not as important as his earlier and less obvious efforts on behalf of those he employed. Any conscientious man could see by this time that his workpeople needed a certain amount of light and air, and that cloakrooms were a good idea. Not many saw the need for a relationship with their employees which went beyond the old paternal one. And of the few who realized the value of such a relationship fewer still managed to put their ideas into practice.

Joseph's achievement was possible because, inside his factory, his personal influence was immense. It is said that he never lost his temper and seldom gave a direct order. 'Should not this be——?' was a familiar beginning if he discovered something or someone in need of correction. Yet his authority was unquestioned. It was like the discipline of some gifted schoolteachers, to whom the idea of insubordination has never occurred.

He had, also, the confidence of his workpeople. They were not inclined to be suspicious of changes and innovations. This was important, for a hundred years of industrial history had not given employees as a whole much reason to trust those who directed their labours. Many early welfare arrangements and profit-sharing schemes were condemned by those who might have benefited by them as 'only another dodge to get more work out of us'. Sometimes this was a true judgement, sometimes not; but even the most impeccable projects seldom succeeded in factories where there was no trust in the management.

There is a phrase often spoken by men who worked with Joseph. They talk of the 'J. R. Spirit', using the familiar abbreviation which was customary among his friends. The 'J. R. Spirit' meant something quite definite to these people who knew him, though it has little significance for those who did not. But it underlay, in fact, the industrial policy upon which the whole firm was built.

A book published in 1951 defines a good industrial policy as one which 'should above all things be ethical and completely beyond suspicion. . . . It should supply the power by which men work loyally and harmoniously. To be successful it must be a policy which fulfils the fundamental human needs of both the individual and the working team. Nothing can be substituted for these deep psychological needs—the desire for good personal relationships between working groups, the desire for expression and development of personality and ability, the desire to contribute and co-operate to the fullest extent in the fulfilment of a common purpose'.[1]

[1] V. M. Clarke. *New Times, New Methods, and New Men.*

Joseph would not, perhaps, have used the same terms as the modern expert; but he was, in himself, a remarkable personification of a 'good industrial policy'. His integrity was unquestioned, and his power to inspire loyalty was proverbial. The 'psychological needs' of his workpeople took an equal place in his mind with their more obvious physical requirements. And his ideas percolated through the unlovely buildings at Tanner's Moat. No doubt they did not reach every corner of what was now quite a large business, and perhaps there were many who remained untouched by them. Nevertheless they were powerful enough to set a standard which was recognized and accepted.

It was fortunate for Joseph that his two elder sons were capable and willing interpreters of his ideas. John Wilhelm and Seebohm —who were both made partners in the Firm as soon as they were twenty-one—might not always agree with their father on points of detail, but they looked at human situations in the same way as he did himself. This family element was an important ingredient in the management of the factory, and it was constantly reinforced by the arrival of more and more young Rowntrees. Arnold, a son of Joseph's brother John, came to work at Tanner's Moat in 1892, and Henry Isaac's son Frank followed a year later.

These young men were all much influenced by Joseph, and their upbringing and education made them quick to grasp his intentions. Humanitarianism was in their blood and in their bones. They could hardly have helped looking at people—as persons.

The family current, however, was no one-way stream. Joseph's sons and nephews had plenty of ideas of their own and were never backward in making suggestions. Their observation supplemented his own knowledge about what was going on in the factory, and their ears were close to the ground. They were not slow to say exactly what they thought ought to be done.

It is said, nowadays, that a good information service is indispensable to the smooth running of a business. Strangely enough most people like to know what they are doing, and why. They want to know the reason for any change in procedure; and even more urgently, at a time of crisis, they want to know the plan upon which dismissals will be made.

This was something which did not trouble most nineteenth-century employers at all. Men were employed to work, not to ask questions, and when they were dismissed they were dismissed, and that was the end of the matter.

At Tanner's Moat there was no cut-and-dried method of spreading information but there were plenty of ways in which it could be obtained. The four young Rowntrees were in close touch with Joseph, and so were a number of men who had worked with him for years and were now in key positions. Anything directly concerning their own departments was always, naturally, discussed with them, but it was never difficult for a departmental manager to find out what was happening in other parts of the Firm. He could go to Joseph and get his questions answered at first-hand. There was a direct connection, still, between the master of the business and the people in the work-rooms.

There must have been, from time to time, patches of discontent among Joseph's staff. Their hours were long, their surroundings were gloomy, and much of their work was monotonous. But if they grumbled occasionally there is no record of it, and only once was a formal grievance laid before Joseph.

In the Firm's archives there is still a handwritten document which was presented to him on October 12, 1894. It reads:

'Sir,
    'We, the undersigned employees desire you to consider fairly the following resolutions:

'(1) The removal of our present Foreman Manager and a more experienced man to be in his place.

'(2) A fair rate of wages to be paid for work done in this department; that is, the rate per hundred trays to be fixed so as to raise the present standard of wages above ordinary day pay.

'(3) The price we obtain per hundred trays to be handed to the head of this Department for reference.

'(4) To consider the reduction of money for waste.'

There is, unfortunately, no record of how Joseph dealt with this situation; probably he sorted it out in a series of conversations and had no need to put anything down on paper. But he must have seen, in the stilted handwritten manifesto, some of the technical and human questions which were to be an increasing problem as the business developed. The request for payment to be above day pay and on a basis of a 'hundred trays' was probably not difficult to arrange; and very likely it became the basis of bonus systems and piecework in later years. The custom of fining employees for bad work—'waste' was defective chocolate which could not be sold—was already being abandoned by many firms. Two years later certain provisions of the Truck Act made fines illegal, but in any case they had already been found rather inefficient as a deterrent.

The human problem was perhaps more difficult to solve than the technical one. Someone had slipped up over that foreman's appointment, and even so early as this it may have occurred to Joseph that a workroom ought to have some say in the choice of the man who was to be their immediate superior. 'Foremen and forewomen', Seebohm Rowntree wrote years later, 'are those with whom the workers come into daily, almost hourly contact. It is they, more than anyone else, who can render a worker's life in the factory agreeable or miserable.'

It is noticeable, however, that Rowntrees' workers in 1894 were not complaining that their foreman was a bully, but that he was inexperienced. They were asking for more efficiency, not for more lenient discipline.

Joseph, all through the years, kept an anxious eye on the standard of his goods. It was conceivable, as the factory grew larger, that an imperfect consignment might be sent out without his being aware of it. He could be tolerant in many ways, but he was fanatical about the quality of his products. 'Have a *nibble*, now and again,' he would say to his office staff; and his own vigilance was unceasing.

Seebohm once ventured to remind his father that a certain wholesale customer was becoming agitated because his order had been delayed. Joseph replied that the delay had been due to an error in manufacturing the goods, and they had had to be scrapped.

'He's been waiting six weeks!' young Seebohm protested.

'And I'm afraid he may still have to wait another fortnight,' Joseph replied, unimpressed. 'But when he does get it, it will be what he ordered.'

Joseph was not a worrier by nature, and apart from the standard of his goods there was only one other thing in the factory about which he was really anxious at this time. It was the age of some of his staff.

The men who had worked at Tanner's Moat in the early days had not all been young even then. Now some were elderly, and some were not really strong enough for a full day's work. But very few of them were in a position to retire. There was no fixed retiring-age in any industry at this period, and people usually went on working as long as possible because they could not afford to stop.

Now, in the middle of the twentieth century, there is much talk about our ageing population. Hospital accommodation is inadequate for old people who are chronic invalids. There is often no one to look after the old who live alone. Pensions are insufficient. But the problem of the twentieth century fades into insignificance beside that of the nineteenth. In fact, then, it was more than a problem; for a large part of the population to be old was plainly a tragedy.

The lucky people who were past work were the ones who had children with whom they could live or who could contribute to their support. A few might have been able to save enough money to last them until they died. For the rest there was only one answer, the Workhouse and a pauper's grave.

Poverty was something Joseph Rowntree understood. He had analysed it scientifically, and he had observed it for himself. He did not like the thought of it creeping up on anyone he knew. In the late eighties he noticed that one of the men who had been with the Firm since its beginning was looking ill. He made some enquiries and the answers were not reassuring.

'I'm worried about that man,' he said to a friend. 'It's a case of mental and physical disintegration. Before long he will be unfit for his work. I must lay out some money for him against his retirement.'

It is likely that more than one man had 'money laid out for him' in this way, though no one knew anything about it. But it was a haphazard makeshift way of going on, and Joseph was not satisfied with it. He began to turn over in his mind the revolutionary idea of a pension scheme, open to all his employees. It would be very expensive to start, and probably difficult to arrange, but it would be in keeping with the scale of his business. At one time it had been all very well for a master to 'make provision' for a few faithful old servants, but now the proportions of the picture had changed. And yet the needs of a thousand people were no different from the needs of ten.

Four thousand people, in fact, were employed by Rowntrees when the Pension Scheme was finally set up in 1906. Nearly everyone was working at Haxby Road by that time, and the last of the old workrooms at Tanner's Moat was about to be closed. No one regretted the old factory. It had never been at all a pleasant or convenient place in which to work. Nevertheless it had seen the first beginnings of nearly all those things without which the fine modern buildings would have been, in Seebohm's words, 'an unfurnished house'.

A photograph of the new factory in 1895 does not show it as a thing of beauty. Low blocks of buildings huddle about one very tall chimney, and are surrounded by a field of rough grass. Everyone had had quite enough of towers at Tanner's Moat, so the original workrooms at Haxby Road were all of one storey only. The departments were moved by degrees, beginning with the Fruit Room and the Gums. In 1897 the new offices were ready, and they were the first part of the Works to be lit by electricity. The factory had its own generating plant, and it was soon called upon to supply not only light but power, since the transmission by shafting proved increasingly difficult as the workrooms spread farther and farther over the ground.

Nevertheless the place was an efficient unit, and was soon served by its own branch railway line. Production increased by leaps and bounds, and in the five years between 1894 and 1899 the number of Rowntrees' employees was again doubled.

Several times, when he was an old man, Joseph said that it had never been his intention that the Cocoa Works should grow so large. But he could hardly have stopped the process once it had begun. He was too good a business man deliberately to check an expanding trade. He did not, however, allow it to overpower him. He made very few changes in his habits or his way of life, and his weekly diversion continued to be a walk at Scarborough on Saturdays.

These 'Saturday walks' were a tradition. The factory had always stopped work at two o'clock on Saturdays, and when it became possible for Joseph to allow himself a little leisure he made it his practice to take the whole day off. His procedure did not vary. He caught the ten o'clock train to Scarborough, drank a cup of coffee at the café owned by his cousin, bought some apples and ginger biscuits, and went for a walk which lasted until four. Rowntree's café saw him again at tea-time, and afterwards he took the train back to York.

Very often, in the early days, his brother John was Joseph's companion on these excursions. They had been good friends all their lives and had worked together for seventeen years in the Pavement shop. But if John could not go, Joseph would invite someone else to share his outing. Sometimes it would be one of his pupils from the Adult School; but more often, as time went one, he would ask one of the factory staff.

There were some who declined the honour. To be alone all day with 'J. R.' seemed to diffident men too much like being invited to spend the day with Royalty. But those who accepted the invitation found that there was, after all, nothing alarming about it. Joseph was quite unself-conscious and never lacked subjects for conversation. Some of his companions may have begun the day nervous and tongue-tied, but they had generally recovered their composure long before Cornelian Bay was reached.

These Saturday walks, begun in early middle age, continued to be Joseph's custom until his death. They may have seemed an odd form of recreation for an important executive, but Joseph was far removed from the accepted pattern of a prosperous man. He bore none of the outward signs of a self-made fortune. A porter at the station always had two foot-warmers ready for him on Saturday mornings, but these were his only concessions to luxury. A thin, rather shabby mackintosh was stuffed into one of his pockets, and apples and ginger biscuits were his chosen lunch to the end of his days. Quiet in speech, unassuming in manner, often slow to come to a decision, more trenchant with pen than with tongue, he may sometimes have misled, quite unconsciously, those who did business with him. Only afterwards, perhaps, when they came to examine the details of a contract, would they realize that they had met someone who in spite of his integrity was more than their equal as a man of business.

CHAPTER TWELVE

DURING the nineteenth century English industry was in an anomalous position. England was known as the workshop of the world, but to be 'in trade' was still something for which many people found it necessary to apologize. A man would sometimes say that he had put his son into business because he was fit for nothing else.

It had not always been so. In the Middle Ages commerce had had its appointed and respected place, and the Merchant Companies had been the real rulers of the City of London. Both the Tudors and the Stuarts had courted the goodwill and respected the power of business men. Pageantry and dignity surrounded the Guilds which governed the ancient business world, and landed gentry who owned sheep-runs could take pride in being also 'Merchants of the Staple'. Younger sons of county families were quite often sent to work for City masters, and not a few rose to be powerful magnates.

The Industrial Revolution changed all this. The first mills, built in remote valleys because they depended on water-power, had no pageantry about them. Their 'apprentices' were very often foundlings, shipped wholesale from London parishes at the age of seven, with some mill-owners agreeing to take one idiot among every twenty children. It was a degradation of the whole apprenticeship system, which, in spite of some bad masters, had been for centuries a good educational and economic beginning to a boy's career.

When the water-powered mills were abandoned and factories were built in towns, the situation was hardly improved. There was legislation to limit women's and children's hours and to safeguard people against dangerous machinery, but no laws could give to the new industries that honourable status which trade had once held in the community. The new manufacturer was often a man of a different stamp from the old-fashioned merchant, and although there were individuals like the elder Peel and the elder Gladstone who were held in great esteem by their contemporaries, they were the exception rather than the rule. Even at the end of the nineteenth century business men were spoken of patronizingly by the landed gentry, the professional classes, and the artistic world, though by then they employed the majority of England's working population.

The new commercial magnates, on the whole, did not care to be patronized. Their background was usually Radical and Nonconformist, and, unlike the old merchants, there had been no coming and going between their families and the aristocracy. A few of them bought estates in the country and set about establishing themselves in county circles, but for the most part they had no respect for profitless hobbies and less for Privilege in any form. They took defiance for their armour and imposed upon themselves what has been described as a deliberate impoverishment of spirit. They were plain men of business and took pride in being nothing else.

In this changing industrial world, however, there were some people whose position remained unaltered. They were the owners of long-established businesses who took their power for granted, and whose social and intellectual life had been comfortably arranged outside the prevailing system. Many Friends were in this category. For generations they had considered themselves a people apart from the 'world' and were not ashamed of being in trade. They did not mix with anyone likely to patronize them, and their traditions made any attempt to 'keep up with the Joneses' practically impossible. They had their own social life within the Society, and their intellectual pursuits had never been dependent on any university. Though their fortunes might improve greatly and their businesses develop into large-scale firms, they seldom made much change in their way of life.

In 1897 Joseph Rowntree was still living in the house his father had built. He employed five women servants and two men, a gardener and a coachman. With four children still living at home it was not a grand establishment by the standards of the time. Even a small shopkeeper's wife normally kept one maid, and a staff of six was not unusual for two people.

Joseph's personal expenditure was on the same scale. His clothes cost him twenty-three pounds in the year 1897; which was, in fact, two pounds less than he had spent twenty years before. His bills for food, fuel, household repairs and redecoration vary little with the years. It is clear that even when he was a comparatively poor young man he had always spent as much as he could afford in keeping his possessions in good repair— carpet-shaking and re-polishing furniture occur regularly in his early accounts—but now that he was wealthy he was not tempted into extravagance. When replacing a drawing-room carpet he might pay twenty-eight pounds instead of eighteen, but it was still his habit to have faded curtains dyed and cut down to fit smaller windows.

His journeys, on the other hand, grew steadily more costly. Sometimes he went abroad twice in the same year, and often he took friends and relations and paid all or part of their expenses. 'Money spent on travel is never wasted,' he said.

Only in one other direction did Joseph's expenditure increase as rapidly as the sums he spent abroad. His subscriptions and contributions to various charities rose from £127 to £816 in ten years.

In 1897 Rowntrees became a limited liability company, and changed its name from H. I. Rowntree & Co. to Rowntree & Co. Ltd. Joseph was the first Chairman of the Board, and the other directors were his sons John Wilhelm and Seebohm, his nephews Arnold and Frank, and Mr J. Bowes Morrell. Arnold's brother, Theodore Rowntree, was appointed Secretary to the Board, so that in one sense it was still very much a family business.

There is a theory in the Army that no chief of general staff should ever have more than six directly subordinate officers, and that five is a better number. It is said that one man cannot supervise efficiently a large team whose work interlocks. No doubt it was by chance that Rowntrees' first directors made up the num-her which Army experts consider ideal, but they were without question a good working unit. Except for Joseph they were all under thirty, and they brought new ideas and young enthusiasm to the management of the company in which most of them had been working since their schooldays.

It was time for new ideas in some directions. Joseph was still conservative about advertisements, and there was no separate advertising department when the Firm became a limited liability company. Even in 1899 only one man is described as 'permanent advertising staff', though two years before this some very spectacular publicity was, in fact, arranged by Arnold Rowntree.

There was a great bond of friendship between Joseph and his young nephew-director. Arnold, in his twenties, had some of the same light-heartedness as Henry Isaac. It was a quality Joseph found endearing. Perhaps only Arnold could have persuaded a man who fundamentally disliked all display to allow one of the first motor-cars ever seen in Yorkshire to be driven about with an enormously magnified tin of 'Elect' cocoa fixed to it.

The car was more like a carriage than a modern vehicle, though it was certainly propelled by an engine. Behind the small driver's seat the cocoa tin looked huge, and in windy weather it had to be sent to its destination by train, since it tended to blow the car over. But it travelled many miles through many towns before it achieved a glorious if involuntary publicity stunt by breaking down in the busiest street in Sheffield. The police were not pleased, but 'Elect' cocoa was certainly a subject of conversation.

Arnold's next venture was equally dramatic. At the Oxford versus Cambridge boat-race in 1897 a barge covered with advertisements for 'Elect' cocoa, and drawn by mechanically propelled swans, sailed majestically down the course. It was definitely noticeable, and Joseph might have winced if he had seen it. But he remained true to his long-established policy of never interfering if he could avoid it in the activities of those to whom he had entrusted a job.

It has been said that there are three critical points in the development of any business. The first comes when the owner or manager has to start delegating full responsibility instead of routine supervision in any major department, the second when he has to delegate all technical control, and the third when he has to co-ordinate his technical experts with his other authorities. The last task is generally the most difficult, and can be achieved only if the head of the business is well aware of the necessity for not allowing other people's conflicts to overwhelm him.

The first critical stage in the development of the Rowntree Firm was simplified by the fact that the younger generation of the family went to work at Tanner's Moat. Joseph did not find it difficult to hand over a good many of his responsibilities to John Wilhelm and Seebohm. The second stage, when it was necessary for him to delegate most of his technical control, does not seem to have presented him with any insuperable problems. Probably it happened gradually, as new machines and new processes were introduced, and no doubt his basic principle of choosing his staff carefully and then giving them a free hand helped him through this period. The third and most exacting task, the co-ordination of technical experts and other people in positions of authority, was successfully carried through because Joseph had many of the qualities of a great statesman.

He was quick to see and anticipate the potential danger-points in a situation. Before any meeting over which he was to preside he studied the agenda and assembled the facts with painstaking thoroughness, arming himself in advance for any troublesome matter which might arise. There was no element of intrigue in his nature, and, in his father's words, he 'wanted no "catchings" but to get to the bottom of the matter'. Nevertheless it was noticeable that anything likely to promote acrimonious discussion was often put late on the agenda. He showed great tact, says one account, in delaying matters that were unprofitable.

Joseph's skill in dealing with people was much appreciated by the various committees upon which he served, but it was in his own business that it was more valuable than anywhere else. For these were the tricky years when improvisation had to make way for expert techniques. The different departments of the factory were becoming specialized, and those who had been responsible for them in their experimental stages sometimes found it hard to accept younger men with more up-to-date methods. Joseph, with his long memories of the past but with his eyes fixed on the future, unobtrusively oiled the wheels of the awkward change-over.

Many family firms put their authority into the hands of salaried managers when they become limited liability companies, and there were some advantages in the practice. A manager was often inclined to try new systems and call in technical experts more willingly than the original owner. There was always the danger that the fortunes of a factory would be marred by the inefficiency of the second generation, or even by the prejudice and obstinacy of the founder himself in his old age. On the other hand a change of management is always unsettling, and no newcomer can get much help from the past. Ancient history is sometimes important in a difficult situation.

Rowntree & Co. had the best of both worlds where management was concerned. Joseph's years of experience had not dimmed his enthusiasm. At an age when many men's minds are encased in the amber of their past achievements he still had a young willingness to try anything which sounded reasonable. His fellow-directors provided him with plenty of opportunities.

Joseph depended a great deal on his sons and his nephews, and on one or two other young men whom he knew well. Their code of ethics was the same as his own, and he listened attentively even to their most daring suggestions. It was a process of cross-fertilization, and no one now can tell how many of Seebohm's theories he owed to his father, or how many of Joseph's projects grew out of discussions with his sons.

John Wilhelm had always been one of Joseph's most intelligent helpers in the factory, but in 1899 he had to leave it. He was only thirty-one, but he was no longer strong enough for daily work. Also he was going blind. At twenty-six he had been told by a specialist that he would inevitably lose his sight before long. Since he was already deaf this was a devastating sentence. He accepted it with great courage and a matter-of-factness which forbade pity. He went on working at Rowntrees, and he continued to stir the Society of Friends with new ideas. But the moment came when he had to retire from business. He went to live in the country, though he continued to be a director and still kept a finger on some of the Firm's social activities.

There were now a great many of these. The long-ago Sunday 'readings' to the apprentices in the Pavement shop, the concerts at the Exhibition Building and the 'social evenings' for the office staff in Joseph's own house—all these were developing into organized clubs and societies. Where once a 'cricket outfit' had been bought by Joseph for the entertainment of a boys' outing to Harrogate Stray, there was now a Cricket Club with a fixture list. There were Singing Classes and Dressmaking Classes, an Angling Society, and Bowling, Camera, Cycling, Football and Tennis Clubs. There was also the 'Bookeries', whose meetings were held fortnightly to discuss poetry and novels and sometimes to read plays.

There were plenty of employees now to keep all these activities going. Once again the firm had doubled its numbers in an even more spectacular way than before; one thousand in 1897, over two thousand in 1902.

Trade was good in those years, and there is no doubt that Arnold's advertising helped the Firm to make the most of it. Before the episodes of the motor-car and the barge at the boat-race, the 'Elect' cocoa staff had consisted of six men, with occasional help from three or four women. Eight years later the department employed permanently two hundred and forty people, and its weekly output had increased from sixteen hundredweight to twenty-six tons.

Other parts of the factory told the same story. The original joiner now had two foremen and a staff of thirty-seven. The engineering department was becoming more important and better equipped, though even from the new factory at Haxby Road it was not uncommon for a man to be 'sent into town to buy bits of steel'. Ten or twelve pounds at sixpence a pound was the usual amount required.

Many things were changing at the Cocoa Works, but one

thing did not change at all. Joseph was still asking the same questions about his employees and their welfare.

He was getting on for seventy now. He could look back over fifty years in business and see the shape of them in historical perspective. Gone was the tradition of obedience to a 'master' which had been handed down from the medieval workshops. Gone was the subjection of unquestioning children and powerless adults in the mills of the Industrial Revolution. Gone too, in most places, was the individual's interest in a small enterprise where he could see the result of his efforts. What remained? What was the shape of things to come for the three thousand people in his factory? Their anonymity alarmed him. He had no contact with the majority of them, but his sense of responsibility remained.

Joseph was always practical, and he took practical steps to see that as far as possible there should be no 'cogs in a machine' attitude in his business. He had found welfare-workers useful, and more were appointed as the number of his employees increased. There were seven in 1904, three men and four women, which was a large number by comparison with the eight departmental managers at the same date.

More important than the welfare-workers, however, was Joseph's very careful choice of men to fill positions of responsibility. Such appointments were only made after much consideration of the work and the workers in a particular department, and also of the personality of the man who was to be in charge of them. It was Joseph's practice to make a scientific analysis of the job itself, and then to dissect the character, temperament, and ambitions of the person applying for it.

'Will you find what you really want in that department? Will it be a satisfying occupation for you, I wonder?'

These were the sort of questions he would discuss, on a Saturday's walk at Scarborough, with young men at a cross-roads of their career; and one of them remembers thinking that no one had ever taken so much trouble over him in his whole life before.

It was good social case-work, and it was good business as well, for Joseph's young executives became leaders in their own right, once he was assured that they were properly placed. They were not fussed by constant commands and prohibitions from above; and Joseph himself was left with the relatively uncluttered desk which is essential for progress.

Perhaps this capacity for true delegation was one of the main reasons for the extraordinarily rapid growth of the business after its difficult early years, for unless a man can shed some of his responsibilities his firm must remain a small one. There is a definite point beyond which no single person's initiative and authority can go, and as there were now what Joseph describes as three 'separate mills', his position would have been impossible without a band of subordinates upon whom he could depend absolutely.

The fact that the business, for sixteen years, was carried on partly at Tanner's Moat and partly at Haxby Road, presented some administrative difficulties; but there were other less clear-cut problems. Departments were becoming units of their own now and there was less and less coming and going between them. Even workshops in the same building often had little contact with each other.

This worried Joseph. He had been bred in a religious Society whose method of worship depended on a group of people. He had spent all his early working life with small units of workmen. He knew and valued that curiously comfortable and intimate feeling which can grow up even among incongruous personalities when they are engaged in a common task. And he feared that it was being lost in the increasing size of his business.

Here he anticipated the industrial psychologists. The relationships between person and person and between group and group are now recognized as factors in production, but they were not often taken into account by expanding firms in the early nineteen hundreds. 'We don't bother about co-ordination and all that, we tell people what to do and they have to do it', was a phrase which could still, in fact, be heard in 1938.

But to Joseph, in 1902, the divisions within his business seemed too important to be ignored. When he started the *Cocoa*

Works Magazine in March of that year it was a deliberate attempt to close some of the gaps.

He wrote in the first issue: 'The increasing number of those who are associated with the Cocoa Works—more than two thousand—makes it impossible to keep up a personal acquaintance with the staff as fully as was the case in the earlier years of the business. . . . The work is carried on in three mills instead of one, and even in the separate mills it becomes more and more departmental, so that those in one room may see little of those who are working in other rooms.

'This change, I know, is inevitable. But if the business is to accomplish all that the Directors desire in combining social progress with commercial success, the entire body of workers must be animated by a common aim, and this will surely be furthered by a periodical devoted to matters of common interest.'

It is not easy to judge whether the *Magazine* fulfilled Joseph's hopes for it, but in some ways it was a remarkable publication. There were very few 'house journals' in England at this time, and the firms who did introduce them generally confined themselves to articles of technical interest, statements on production in different departments, and anecdotes from commercial travellers about their success in selling twice as much blacklead or boot-polish as they had done the year before. Such magazines could hardly have been duller.

The *Cocoa Works Magazine*, under its first editor, Mr Crichton, broke new ground. Unlike most of its few contemporaries, it was well printed on good paper. There was, naturally, much topical factory news in it. The activities of clubs and societies were regularly reported, and staff deaths, marriages, and promotions had their due place. But there were also book reviews, travel diaries, articles on Scott's Antarctic expedition, 'impressions' of the House of Commons, and notes on local history. There were photographs, poems, and occasionally a really witty parody in the style of Sherlock Holmes or some other well-known character of fiction. Even in its early days the *Magazine* recognized that its readers might have interests beyond the Cocoa Works—or that they ought to have. It was a strangely different attitude from the trade magazines in which the 'story-ettes' all pointed a commercial moral and had plots revolving around the virtues of a particular brand of tin-tacks or tea.

'The change, I know, is inevitable,' Joseph wrote in his letter to the *Magazine.* Was there a little regret in the words, or were they simply a statement of fact? He had known so many changes, not all of them for the better, not all of them fulfilling what they had promised. Free education, public libraries, the cleaning and draining of towns, votes for all men, penny postage, much legislation for the 'under-dog'—he had seen all this, and much more, achieved within his conscious memory. He was the last person to sigh for the good old days. Yet, in this better world of the twentieth century, something was missing.

'Compared with their fathers the men of this time were ceasing to be a ruling and a reasoning stock. . . . Fundamentally what failed, in the late Victorian age, and its flash Edwardian epilogue, was the Victorian public, once so alert, so masculine, and so responsible.'[1]

Perhaps Joseph had begun to feel this, as he studied the younger generations of his workpeople, and compared them with the old. Now, looking out of the window of his new office, he saw a garden; and walking through the new factory he noticed the spaciousness and the cheerful light of the workrooms. They were a splendid contrast to Tanner's Moat. He had provided as satisfactory a setting as possible for his employees' working day, but he was well aware that his task did not end here. 'There are some things better than good rooms and pleasant gardens,' he said.

He remembered the anxious, crowded years in the old factory, the triumph of difficulties overcome, the demands made upon his workmen in a moment of crisis, and the shared satisfaction when an unexpected order was dispatched in a hurry. There had been, in those days, a good deal more than a man's wages to hold his interest in his work. There should be something more now, though the clock could not be turned back, and no one could whip up excitement to order. In a modern setting it was out of

[1] G. M. Young. *Victorian England. Portrait of an Age.*

Factory at Tanner's Moat in the nineties

'North Street' workshop (adjoining Tanner's Moat) in the nineties

8]

7 Joseph Rowntree with (left to right) Stephen Rowntree, Seebohm Rowntree, Arnold Rowntree, and Oscar Rowntree, May 31, 1923

Joseph Rowntree and the Very Reverend Dean Purey-Cust, receiving the freedom of the city, 1911

place and undesirable. Yet no doubt there were still undiscovered resources of skill and ingenuity in the factory, as there had been when an emergency called them out in earlier days. He decided to establish a Suggestions Scheme.

It was a mild unromantic idea, but it was an innovation in the industrial world of the time. The details were given in the *Magazine* in 1902.

Prizes were offered for suggestions:

'(1) For improved methods of manufacturing or packing goods, and for improvements in the quality of goods.

'(2) For quicker or more economical methods of manufacture, or of carrying on any work undertaken by the Firm.

'(3) For improvements in machinery, etc.

'(4) For improvements in the conditions under which work is conducted.

'(5) Any other matters which affect the welfare of the Firm and of the Employees.

'Prizes [the amount of which was specified] are offered for the best suggestions actually adopted, or accepted for adoption. . . . Anything, *no matter how small*, will come under this head.'

The italics are in the original notice.

The scheme had a slow start. Workers were chary of making suggestions at first, thinking that their immediate superiors might regard such an action as a criticism of their own abilities. But when it was stressed that a good suggestion reflected credit on the whole group from which it came, people grew bolder. Year after year, in the *Magazine*, there are photographs of prize-winners. They are male and female, old men who had worked for years at Tanner's Moat, boys who had recently left school, pretty girls and formidable-looking women. They have nothing in common but this—that they had exercised their imagination or their ingenuity or their common sense on behalf of the Firm.

CHAPTER THIRTEEN

'POWERS that have been quickened by a business training may usefully be turned in other directions,' Joseph said in one of his memoranda; and he added that the discipline acquired in mastering the details of a business will be found valuable in other occupations.

All his life Joseph had done a great deal of public work. At twenty-three he had taken his father's place on the committee responsible for the two Quaker schools in York. For a solid forty-two years he served on the committee which governed the mental hospital known as The Retreat, and was its chairman for much of that time. He was the founder of the modern Liberal Association in York, and its chairman for a long period. He had been one of the governors of York's only undenominational school, the British School in Hope Street. He had helped to establish the city's public library. And every Sunday morning, until he was over sixty, he took his class in the Adult School.

Many of these activities were in the established Quaker traditions and few Friends of Joseph's age and standing could easily have avoided them. But his range of interests did not lie wholly within the Society. When the appointment of a board of directors relieved him of some of his responsibility he turned with all the gusto of a young man to the world beyond the factory. And there he saw what he had seen thirty years before—Poverty.

In 1892 Charles Booth had published a book called *The Life and Labour of the People of London*. It was a formidable indictment of conditions in the East End, and showed statistically that thirty per cent of the population were paupers. Booth's figures may be questioned by modern statisticians, but the size of the problem itself was beyond all argument. In the capital city of a prosperous country there were a million people who had, even by the lowest standards, not enough to eat. The average London working-man with more than three children could not earn enough to provide his family with a diet as good as that of the Workhouse. And Workhouse food was recognized as inadequate for anyone doing hard manual work, or for growing children.

But if the poor could not eat, they could, and did, drink. Booth only attributed fourteen per cent of his cases of poverty to alcohol, though he adds: 'It is only as a principal cause that drink is here considered; as a contributory cause it would no doubt be connected with a much larger proportion.'

Perhaps it was that sentence which started Joseph off again on his pursuit of statistics. The words 'contributory cause' were a challenge to one whose passion for tracing things back to their roots had not lessened with the years. He enlisted the help of Mr Arthur Sherwell, who was interested in social studies, and together they began to plan the book which was to be called *The Temperance Problem and Social Reform*.

A distrust of alcohol had been instilled into Joseph in his childhood.

'My father was an able man, and one who kept very close to the facts of life in his thinking,' Joseph wrote in a little article addressed to his own grandchildren. 'In his youth it was the custom for almost everyone to take beer to meals, and it was supplied to the young men in the Pavement shop when they dined with my father and mother in the middle of the day. But my father said to himself that if these young men get into the habit of taking alcohol one or more of them is almost certain to be mastered by it sooner or later, and become a drunkard. . . . He therefore discontinued the use of beer himself and banished it from his table.'

This was a very strange action in the eighteen-twenties, when even the Society of Friends had not yet displaced alcohol from its position as one of the 'good creatures of God'. Moderation was the only thing then considered necessary. Even the wild gin-drinking of the early eighteenth century had drawn from Friends no more than a recommendation to 'watchful care against the prevalent excess'; and not until 1835 was there any suggestion that it might be desirable to abstain completely from distilled spirits.

The earliest advocates of temperance drew a sharp distinction between spirits and wine or beer. The latter were considered innocuous if drunk with discretion, and Joseph himself bought four dozen bottles of light wine as late as 1867, and had them shipped from Hamburg to York with his second wife's belongings. Until 1880 a few bottles of wine and beer are entered in his domestic accounts every year. The beer and porter may perhaps have been bought for the nurse who attended his wife during her confinements, and the sherry and port could have been for use in cooking; but it is difficult to explain the purchase of a dozen bottles of champagne in 1874 unless one assumes that Joseph had not then been persuaded that alcohol in every form was undesirable.

By the time he began to plan his book, however, Joseph was in complete agreement with his father's beliefs; and also with those of Joseph Livesey, the first advocate of total abstinence, who had persuaded seven other men to sign the original pledge of 1832.

Public opinion on the subject of temperance was not easily changed. The old admiration for a man who could drink hard and hold his liquor like a gentleman did not disappear quickly. Eighteenth-century Parliaments, which had more than once had to adjourn early because members were too drunk to do business, found their echo in late nineteenth-century mayors' banquets, where it was not uncommon for an alderman to be under the table before the end of the evening. Even in York itself a Town Clerk sometimes met his committees 'in a state of approaching intoxication'. No social stigma attached to such occurrences for a very long time.

It was generally recognized that ladies should not get drunk, and that gentlemen should only do so when they were on their own (hence the practice of women retiring to the drawing-room after dinner and leaving the men to their port), but on the whole the drinking-habits of the upper classes went uncriticized. 'As drunk as a lord' was a phrase which held more envy than censure.

The drunkenness of the poor was another matter. They did not carry their liquor in a civilized manner. Nor could they afford it. It destroyed their efficiency as workers. And this, as the Industrial Revolution got into its stride, was serious.

The poor had been drinking hard for two hundred years by the time Joseph began to write his book. Smollett, early in the eighteenth century, had seen the 'painted boards inviting people to be drunk for the small expense of one penny, and assuring them that they might be dead drunk for tuppence, and have straw to lie on for nothing'. In these two centuries several attempts had been made to check the intemperance of the poor. The licensing system, which had been in existence in one form or another since 1552, was revised again and again. Duties and taxes were imposed, and altered, and increased. Desperate expedients were tried. In 1729 Parliament restricted the sale of gin to publicans who paid the enormous yearly sum of £50 for a licence. Only two such licences were ever taken out, for in those days fifty pounds was a great deal of money, but nevertheless the amount of gin manufactured rose by over two million gallons in eight years. The law was ignored and the poor went on drinking. In due course the law had to be revised.

In 1830 the Chancellor of the Exchequer in the Duke of Wellington's ministry tried another experiment. He removed the taxes on beer and cider, and allowed both to be sold without a publican's licence. Any rate-payer could now open his house as an ale-house by paying two guineas to the local office of excise. It was optimistically prophesied that this would reduce the consumption of spirits, and lead to 'general temperance among the labouring classes'.

But the poor went on drinking, and on the whole continued to prefer the gin-shop, which now rose 'like a palace' to challenge the hundreds of tiny squalid beer-houses. 'Free Trade in Beer', as it was sometimes called, proved to have none of the advantages which had been claimed for it, though it lasted for nearly forty years, and was only stopped by an Act of Parliament in 1869.

In 1897, when Joseph and Mr Sherwell started their investigation, the very poor were still drinking much as they had done in Smollett's day.

The Temperance Problem and Social Reform is not an attractive title. One can hardly imagine anyone but a student or a social worker taking it eagerly from the library shelves. Yet, oddly enough, it was a best-seller. There were six editions published in the first eight months, two more in the next year, and a cheap edition in 1901. Altogether about ninety thousand copies were sold.

The reviews were impressive. The *Daily Chronicle*, in a leading article, said: 'We have never seen the problems of drink and human misery more clearly or dispassionately reviewed.' The *Daily News* observed that this was 'no intemperate and uncompromising tract, but a book of really interesting facts and figures'. Even *The Times* noted that 'here is an invaluable compendium of authentic information'.

It was certainly a compendium. Beginning with an analysis of wages, rents, and the cost of food, Joseph and Mr Sherwell discovered that the working-man spent between four and six shillings a week on drink. Their figures were gathered with the 'assistance of a number of helpers in different centres', and were checked by the estimates of experts on taxation, by government reports, and by conversations with bar-tenders, schoolmasters, and foremen in factories. They were not challenged. It was apparently undeniable that a large proportion of the men who lived constantly on the edge of poverty further jeopardized their position by spending about one-sixth of their income on beer and spirits. It was, indeed, a problem.

Before offering any ideas towards its solution Joseph and Mr Sherwell surveyed in some detail the situation in other countries. From the 'dry' states in America they collected facts about Prohibition, and from Russia information about the Government Monopoly of Spirits. They investigated the 'Company System' in Sweden and Norway—a system of employing salaried managers who got no profit from the sale of alcohol. In an appendix they note that there has been an 'increase in late years in the consumption of alcohol in France'; though the statistics as to the number of *petits verres* (sic) drunk daily by the French were unfortunately *not* accurate enough to be of much value.

As a result of these foreign investigations, checked in America by Mr Sherwell and in Scandinavia by his own personal visits, Joseph came to certain conclusions. The first was that it would be not only useless but also unwise to attempt any kind of total prohibition in England. The state of Maine had tried it in 1851. A law prohibiting the sale or consumption of any sort of alcoholic liquor, and described as the 'pattern law of prohibition', had been passed by the State Senate in that year. In 1856 it had been repealed, but it was reimposed in 1858. When Mr Sherwell went to America Maine had been consistently 'dry' for forty years; but as he took an evening walk through the city of Portland he was able to visit forty saloons in a couple of hours. They did not advertise the sale of liquor, but there was no attempt to hide it. Nor did the proprietors object when a professional photographer was engaged by Mr Sherwell to take pictures of the interior of various bars. They were all lawbreakers and entirely secure in their illegal position.

Sixteen other states in America had passed some form of prohibitive Act during the second half of the nineteenth century, but by 1899 only seven states remained 'dry'. And in the larger towns in all these states the law was openly flouted.

Joseph and Mr Sherwell naturally regarded this as an unsatisfactory state of affairs, and one which provided no solution to their problem. There was more hope in Scandinavia.

Sweden, in 1865, had tried an experiment in the town of Gothenburg. A company had been formed to take over all the bars in which spirits were sold. This company put managers into its establishments and paid them a fixed salary. All profits belonged to the company, and were turned over to the town treasury after a small dividend had been paid on the capital originally put up by 'twenty highly respected firms and individuals'. There was no personal profit for the men who actually sold the liquor.

The same plan was tried out in many other Swedish towns, and a similar sort of 'company system' was adopted by Norway. In England the People's Refreshment House Association and the Public-House Trust Companies were both modelled on the

135

Gothenburg system, and the elimination of private profit was their first principle.

Joseph and Mr Sherwell regarded the 'company system' as a success—or at least as much of a success as one could expect in an imperfect world. It was certainly a fact that the consumption of spirits went down both in Sweden and in Norway, though a certain increase in beer-drinking was also apparent, for beer-houses did not come under the company's control and remained open much later than the company's bars. But in England the 'Gothenburg' public-houses did not seem likely to revolutionize the Englishman's drinking habits. The tea and coffee which were so readily available, the banishing of all advertisements for alcohol, the fact that managers were generally given all profits on soft drinks and nothing on alcohol—none of these things made very much difference to the men who liked their liquor.

'The customer comes in with his order on his lips,' as one bartender said, 'and no manager, when an order for beer or whisky is given, can *easily* suggest that his client should take lemonade instead.'

But in spite of all these difficulties and drawbacks Joseph felt sure that the establishment of some form of company system was essential. As long as the liquor trade remained in private hands the man who sold drink would try to sell as much of it as possible. He was a business man himself, and this seemed to him obvious.

Joseph had an outstanding ability to do a thing *properly*. Whether he was running a factory, laying out a garden, endowing a trust, or writing a book, he took pains to assemble his forces and consider the demands of the task before him. There was a calm self-respecting sense of quality in his methods. Much time was spent in planning and arranging whatever job was on hand. In many ways he was like an old-fashioned craftsman laying out his tools slowly and carefully before embarking on a piece of work. The result was an absence of amateurishness in an age when it was very easy to be an amateur.

Joseph's first book reflects this quality and it sold because it was topical, dispassionate, and packed with facts instead of pious reflections. There were no appeals to anyone's better nature in it, no preaching, and very little censure except upon financial grounds. It was the work of a practical man, saying 'You can't afford it'; and of a realist who saw that everyone *would* afford it unless something else was found to supply their need.

I do not know if Joseph went into many public-houses in the course of his investigation. I am quite sure that he himself never drank a glass of spirits, though he knew to a decimal of a cubic centimetre the difference between an English 'dram' and one poured out in America or in Sweden. But he was well aware of the reasons why men took to alcohol.

'Man is a social being', he observes, 'and he desires converse with his fellows. But he cannot invite a friend to spend a social evening at his house when that house is a tenement where one room must serve all the family as kitchen, wash-house, sitting-room, bedroom, nursery, and perhaps workroom as well.'

It was not an exaggerated description. Ten years earlier a Government report had stated that between one-half and one-third of the urban population of England were living in conditions 'incompatible with the most elementary claims of decency, health, or morality'. There had been a Royal Commission on housing since that Government report, and a new Housing Act had been passed. But in fact not many new houses had been built, and even the rents of these were too high for workmen with large families. The poor, as well as being under-nourished, were frequently still living six to a room. It was hardly surprising that they turned to the brightly lighted gin-palaces and the warm little beer-houses for comfort.

But there were other reasons for the popularity of the public-house. 'It is necessary to understand the conditions under which people *work*, as well as those in which they live,' Joseph writes, and this was a subject he knew more about than most men. He had spent thirty years in a factory, and he had no illusions about the factory system.

'Machinery has made men's work less physically exhausting,' he observes, 'but the conditions of labour are still extremely irksome. There is often incessant noise, noxious heat, and dust-laden air. *Above all* there is a nervous tension and an extreme monotony. The attraction of the public-house, as a relaxation from these things, can easily be imagined.'

This was a new approach to the problem of drunkenness. Everybody knew that for the very poor drink was 'the quickest way out of Manchester'; but no one before Joseph had suggested that the slightly more prosperous also found in alcohol the fastest escape from the boredom of their jobs.

Was there nothing but drink which could help those whose living conditions were disgusting, or whose work was frustratingly monotonous?

Joseph thought there was. 'People's Palaces' were his answer, and he considered that one ought to be built in every sizeable town. If all the public-houses in the country were run on a 'company system' there would soon be enough profit from them to finance the People's Palaces; and in the meantime a Government grant should be given to meet a situation which had been growing steadily more intolerable since the Industrial Revolution turned England into a nation of town-dwellers.

The phrase 'People's Palace' sounds curiously in modern ears, for the word 'people' is no longer used to describe the lower-income groups, and a palace is where the Queen lives, or else the local cinema. But in 1899 there were, in fact, two such Palaces in existence, one in East London and one in Glasgow. They were a combination of art gallery, concert hall, and winter garden, and they were both situated in slum areas and were well patronized. The price of admission was twopence.

In Joseph's ideal Palaces there was to be provision for all tastes: really *good* lectures on widely varying subjects for the young and intelligent, simple music for those who were too tired to do anything but sit, and plenty of temperance cafés and 'promenades' where girls and boys could walk and talk and do their courting.

It was a splendid vision—but nothing ever came of it. There were too many obstacles in the way. The most insuperable was that it was financially impossible for the Government (even if it wished to do so) to buy up the liquor trade and pay compensation to the brewers and the pub-keepers.

Joseph and Mr Sherwell wrote four other books in the next seven years. They were called *British 'Gothenburg' Experiments*, *Public Control of the Liquor Traffic*, *Public Interest or Trade Aggrandisement* and *The Taxation of the Liquor Trade*. They are all distinguished by the same dispassionate attitude to the questions discussed, and by the same meticulous checking of facts and figures. Unwelcome conclusions, unexplained mysteries, are all set down as fairly and plainly as possible. No attempt is made to disguise the fact that in certain localities a 'Gothenburg' public-house undoubtedly increased the consumption of alcohol, because it was a clean, comfortable place where respectable people would go when they would never consider frequenting an ordinary tavern. Nor is an explanation offered for the fact that in one 'Gothenburg' public-house the consumption of soft drinks was less under the new manager, who got the profit on them, than it had been under his beer-peddling predecessor. These things did not strengthen their argument, but Joseph and Mr Sherwell faithfully recorded them. Facts, to them, were facts, and they were painting a picture as well as arguing a case.

This objective attitude seems calm and convincing, but it was not altogether welcome to some other adherents of the Temperance Movement. Nor was Joseph's contention that the first step must be some form of public control of the liquor trade by any means accepted by all those who wished to see drunkenness abolished.

The Temperance Movement, in fact, was a house divided even before Joseph and Mr Sherwell began to collect their statistics. Joseph Livesey, who had worked hard for 'The Cause' all his life, remained convinced to the end that only by individual example and personal conviction could the demon of liquor be conquered. 'Buyers are equally to blame with sellers of drink,' he said, 'and forty times as numerous. Let themselves and their jugs keep at home, and there is an end of the Trade. . . . It is not the publican that has dominion over the people, it is their own love of liquor.'

But there were others who took the view that Livesey's methods were too slow and too uncertain. The United Kingdom Alliance, founded in 1853 'to procure the Total and Immediate Legislative Suppression of the Traffic in all Intoxicating Liquors', concentrated on prohibition rather than persuasion. The liquor trade was a wicked business, they argued, and it would be wrong for any Government to countenance the evil by controlling and administering it. Let drink be swept out of the country and there would be no more drunkenness.

Between these opposing factions Joseph appears coolly drawing up tables of figures, and assessing the strength and weakness of the Temperance Movement with the matter-of-factness of a business man. He saw that it would take generations of persuasive methods to sway public opinion to any noticeable extent. He had no faith at all in the idea that if a Permissive Bill were passed large areas of England would abolish their public-houses overnight. Nor could he agree with the 'abolitionists' who were pressing for legislation on the lines of the Maine Law. He had discovered what that led to in Maine itself. His plea was for a measure of 'Local Option' so that those places which genuinely had a large majority of abstainers might be able to close their taverns and drink-shops; and in other districts he would have liked to see state or municipal control of the liquor trade.

He was, even in this cause about which he felt so strongly, entirely realistic. The statistics which he had gathered told their own story. Drunkenness could not be suppressed by law; and it appeared that even a 'dry' district's best chance of staying 'dry' was to have a safety-valve in the shape of an unreformed area within easy walking distance.

Even without total prohibition, however, he believed that much might be done to combat the dangers of alcohol if the reformers could only agree among themselves. 'Union is essential to success,' he says in the preface to *The Temperance Problem and Social Reform*, 'but this elementary proposition has hitherto had little place in the counsels of the Temperance party.'

He appealed for the 'wider outlook, the statesmanship quick to discern the full strength of the forces which may be marshalled'. But, like the People's Palaces, this was too much to ask.

None of the different factions in the nineteenth-century Temperance Movement got what they wanted, but some measure of success may fairly be claimed by them all. Livesey's creed that the reformation of the individual is the first necessity lives on in the work of the modern 'Alcoholics Anonymous'. The United Kingdom Alliance saw the Local Option clause turned down by the House of Lords with the Licensing Bill of 1908; but Scotland carried through a Local Option Act in 1912 and many Scottish parishes and wards of towns have voted 'no-licence' consistently for years. Joseph's hopes of a 'company system' and state control were never nationally adopted, but during the First World War the Government took over the whole of the liquor trade in the Carlisle area and still controls it today. The experiment sufficiently impressed a Royal Commission on Licensing for them to recommend that it should be tried out in other areas. But financial reasons made this suggestion impracticable—it was 1932 when it was made—and Joseph's scheme has now joined many others in the honourable limbo of sound ideas too expensive to be tested.

'It is Time, not argument, which shall arbitrate betwixt us,' Livesey wrote, when he was an old man involved in a disagreement with the United Kingdom Alliance. Time has not arbitrated yet. Reformers have still to prove whether prohibition or persuasion is the more effective and permanent remedy for drunkenness. Nevertheless, one thing stands out above all the arguments; the English are a much more sober nation than they were in 1899.

It is difficult to say precisely how much alcoholism has declined, because the statistics of 'persons proceeded against for drunkenness' have been arranged in two different ways in the course of these fifty-odd years. Such estimates, also, do not show the whole picture. They measure only public incapability, and take no account of persistent mild intoxication or of quiet tippling by the domestic fireside. It is, perhaps, the change in certain customs which shows most clearly how much has been achieved. The public-house is not what it was in Joseph's day. There are no more 'long pulls' to attract customers. There are no bribes of sweets to induce children to take the family jug to the 'Fox' instead of the 'Oak'. No longer, at the gates of a factory, do the bars open at five-thirty in the morning and set each man's glass of spirits ready for him to drink before he begins work. In engineering shops and at factory benches the word 'fetcher' is not even remembered, though once it was common practice for beer to be brought into a workroom whenever it was demanded.

This is the matter-of-fact record, showing plainly through the dust of the long-ago arguments between high-minded men; and in its achievement Joseph's and Mr Sherwell's patient investigations can fairly claim to have played their part. The increasing cost of alcohol and the shorter opening hours of public-houses, both helped the temperance cause; but perhaps, in the end, the most powerful factor was the abolition of that hopeless inescapable poverty from which drunkenness was a welcome though temporary release.

CHAPTER FOURTEEN

IT is tempting to trace connections. In 1822 the Merchant Adventurers' Company of York gave, as was their custom, a 'wine-party' to celebrate the admission of a new member. The new member was the elder Joseph Rowntree, then a young man of twenty-one, who had just bought the shop in Pavement. The Merchant Adventurers became hilarious in their cups, and the elder Joseph put on his hat and left the party in disgust, taking with him a 'distrust of alcohol in all its forms'.

Seventy-five years later this distrust of alcohol led to his son's book on temperance. And some of the facts and figures gathered in the course of preparing that book were used in his grandson Seebohm's classic work, *Poverty. A Study of Town Life*.

Seebohm used many of the statistics which Joseph had collected for *The Temperance Problem and Social Reform* and he was helped by some of the same 'investigators', but his object was to analyse the cause of poverty instead of the menace of alcohol. It is an odd coincidence that he was exactly the same age— twenty-eight—as Joseph had been when he wrote his essay on 'British Civilization', sitting in the counting-house in Pavement and working out his statistics about pauperism.

Seebohm's book was a remarkable achievement for a young man. He confined his enquiry to York, and within the city boundaries he and his investigators visited every single working-class household. He says that he wished to discover, among other things, the true measure of poverty in the city, and 'how much of it was due to insufficiency of income, and how much to improvidence'. He discovered this and much more. And he devised a 'human needs' standard for measuring poverty which was still used, directly or indirectly, in all the many social surveys made between 1921 and 1939.

It has been said that Seebohm's *Poverty* and Booth's *Life and Labour of the People of London* laid the foundations of the Welfare State. Certainly between them they showed unmistakably where most of the trouble lay. The majority of those in poverty were children, the old, the sick, and the unemployed, and Seebohm, at least, was convinced that no improvement in wages would abolish childhood poverty without the addition of family allowances.

John Wilhelm, when he was once asked 'Which Rowntree are *you?*' replied lightly, 'Oh, the brother of Poverty and the son of Drink'.

No doubt this immediately placed him, as far as the enquirer was concerned, but the question is understandable. The Rowntrees were now a large clan, and they hung together. They made up family parties to go abroad, and it was not unusual to find a dozen or more relations staying in the same hotel at Cannes or at Mürren. Even for less ambitious holidays they would often take adjoining lodgings at Whitby or at Scarborough.

At home in Top House family life was also on a large scale. Joseph had now taken over again that smaller piece of the house in which he had begun his married life, and there was plenty of room for visitors. The dining-room could hold twenty people comfortably, and quite often did.

It was a household which carefully avoided, still, any kind of ostentation; but it enjoyed some things which an earlier generation would certainly have thought 'worldly'. There was a tennis court laid down by Joseph on a piece of ground which he had rented from a neighbour. There was a billiard-table. A few pictures were bought from time to time, and fifty pounds was paid for a good piano. But it was, after all, half a century since Joseph's father, influenced by the Quaker feeling of his time against all worldly distractions, had defined the occasions when music was permissible as, 'the lawful, the unlawful—and the expedient'.

In practical matters Joseph was very up to date. He had electricity installed in 1901, and a telephone a year later. All his

8 Joseph Rowntree at
Scarborough, 1912

oseph Rowntree at Scarborough, 1920

9 The Four Generations: Joseph Rowntree, his son, grandson, and great-grandson

family were provided with bicycles, boys and girls alike. He bought a modern one for himself and paid fifteen pounds for it. It was called the Engineer's Patent Safety Model.

Both Joseph and his wife were methodical. In common with many of their generation, they liked to have a 'routine'. Even when on holiday they would map out their days, arranging to walk in the morning, drive in the afternoon, and read aloud after dinner. At home Antoinette's household was run with beautiful order and precision; and the number of things which Joseph fitted into his day without hurrying himself or anyone else bear witness to his skill in organizing his time and energy. There came a moment, however, when the writing of his book on temperance called for more solitude than was easily to be found in Top House. He retreated first of all to a summer-house in the garden, which he called his 'Temperance Den', and finally to the village of Westow, eleven miles from York. Here he rented a house to which he could go when he wanted to concentrate on his books, and in which he could enjoy uninterrupted conversations with those who helped him to write them.

Westow was the only village in which Joseph ever lived, and although he never spent more than two or three consecutive weeks there he had a foothold in the place. He took a seven years' lease of his house, and in that time he learned a good deal about his country neighbours. The parson called on him, and so did the Wesleyan minister. The schoolmistress welcomed his occasional visits to the school. At cottage gates and in the village street he talked to the men whose living came from the land, and the women who wrestled with housekeeping in inconvenient cottages. He savoured, for the first time, some of the essence of village life.

It has been said that for generations English sentiment clung around the village as Roman sentiment clung to the Sabine farm; much was written about the beauty of country life, and the value of the homely wisdom gained from close contact with nature. Joseph, although he was a townsman, had no such romantic feelings. A picturesque cottage had no virtue in his eyes if it was also damp and dark. He could imagine farm work being as hard as factory work, even if it was more varied. What he came to value, in the country, was something more intangible—the corporate life of the village itself. He saw that the inhabitants of Westow were a close community, whether they liked it or not.

To be a 'little world, close-packed and insulated like ants in an ant-hill, or bees in a hive, or sheep in a fold, or nuns in a convent, or sailors in a ship'[1] may have had disadvantages, but also possessed compensations. The villages of Joseph's day were little units of their own, without many contacts beyond their parish boundaries. People were obliged to take some interest in each other, and some responsibility for their neighbours. Class distinctions were as rigid as anywhere else, but there were common interests to make them less obvious. The same weather affected the farmer's fields and the cottager's garden; and the cricket team, of necessity, often included both the squire's son and the boy whose mother was 'on the parish'.

Joseph found much to approve of in village life, and contrasted it thoughtfully with his own city of York. The survey made by Seebohm for his book had shown that York's housing situation, though not nearly as bad as that of many towns, was certainly in need of improvement. Twelve per cent of the working-class population were living in 'back-to-back' houses, often set around airless medieval courtyards; and there were slum areas which were said by experts to be filthier than any in London, even though they were not as large.

The more respectable houses, inhabited by two-thirds of York's working-men, were not very inspiring. Built with thin walls of damp-absorbing bricks, put together with inferior mortar, and with wood so green that floors, window-frames and doors shrank within a year, their fate was obvious. They were the slums of a not-very-distant future. Generally they had no gardens at all, though a few 'well-to-do artisans' living in the newer parts of the city, could boast little railed-in front lawns and a small cemented yard at the back.

Seebohm's book was published at the end of 1901. In the same year Joseph bought one hundred and twenty-three acres border-

[1] Miss Mitford. *Our Village.*

146

ing the land already owned by Rowntree & Co. but a little farther from the city. This was the beginning of the village now called New Earswick, though it was two years before the first site-plan was drawn up.

The history of New Earswick has been written by L. E. Waddi-love in a book called *One Man's Vision*, so it is only necessary to mention it briefly. Garden Cities and Model Villages were much discussed at this time, and several projects had already been started. The Cadbury brothers were building at Bournville, and so was Sir James Reckitt at Hull. At Port Sunlight Sir George Lever had also established a new village, though his houses, un-like Cadbury's and Reckitt's, were only let to his own employees.

The idea that an employer should provide accommodation for his workpeople was not altogether new. In the country it had long been recognized by good farmers that a cottage with a garden was the farm-worker's due. A hundred years before, at the New Lanark mills, Robert Owen had built cottages for his workmen; and a few firms, among them the Arkwrights and the Oldknows, had provided houses and schools for their employees soon after they founded their businesses. In remote districts where coalmining was done mine-owners were frequently obliged to build houses for miners, since no other accommodation was available. But these houses—of which some survived until recent years—were far from being desirable dwellings. There was, throughout the nineteenth century, a general feeling that how or where a workman lived was no concern of his employer's.

New Earswick was a somewhat risky experiment. York was a city of few industries, and often there were a thousand 'reason-ably good' houses in it empty, though the bad cheaper ones never lacked tenants. 'It remains to be seen', wrote Joseph's son See-bohm, 'whether we can build to let at a price people can pay.'

The new housing estate was not designed as a philanthropic enterprise. Nor was it intended that the cottages should be let only to those employed by the Firm. Joseph's ambition was to provide houses 'artistic in appearance, sanitary, well-built, and yet within the means of men earning about twenty-five shillings a week'. It was, in fact, a challenge to bad housing and bad build-

147

ing; and to be an effective challenge it had to earn a return not less than that at which local authorities could borrow for the time being from the Public Works Loan Board. For a large part of the time this was about three and a half per cent.

In the three years between the purchase of the land and the setting-up of a Village Trust, thirty houses were built and let at approximately five shillings a week. Later, when the Trustees came to consider the economic position of the village as a whole, it was discovered that six and a penny was the very least that would have to be charged for cottages of this first type. The Trustees accepted the fact that they would have to reduce their standards if they were to provide anything within the range of the lowest-paid workers—the people with whom Joseph was most concerned. Finally a cottage was designed without a bath-room or a hot-water supply, which could be built for £135 and let at four shillings and sixpence a week. It was not Joseph's ideal but it was an economic proposition, which was important in the circumstances.

More than one type of house was built at New Earswick from the beginning. There were some with baths in the kitchen, some with separate bathrooms, and some with three bedrooms and a parlour. The village was intended for many different sorts and conditions of people.

The Trust Deed definition of possible tenants for the houses in the new village included artisans, shop-assistants, and clerks. But it also included 'all persons who earn their living wholly or partially by the work of their hands or their minds, or earn a small income, and, further . . . persons having small incomes de-rived from invested capital, pensions, or other sources'.

It was a formula capable of wide interpretation, and perhaps designedly so, since Joseph had in his mind the picture of a mixed community such as might be found in any ordinary village in the country. Forty-five years later the same idea worked its way through housing legislation into local government com-mittees. These abolished the phrase 'working-class' and sub-stituted a formula practically identical with Joseph's to be applied to aspiring tenants of their council houses.

Nevertheless, in the beginning, there were drawbacks about New Earswick. The land was flat and uninteresting. The original architect, Raymond Unwin, built his houses in terraces of varying lengths, and curved his service roads to get the maximum both of sunshine and of variety, but there were no trees as yet to disguise the raw newness of the place. Nor were there any buses or street lights, and the roads were rough and full of pot-holes. It must have seemed to many prospective tenants that they were being offered a muddy lonely dump in the country in exchange for the cosiness of the town. The New Earswick houses were invariably far better than any in the city at a comparable rent, but it was only families possessing something of a pioneer spirit who moved into them while the village was in its infancy.

In the fifty-odd years since the first houses were built at New Earswick the village has seen many changes. Additional land has been bought, and accommodation provided for people with very varied requirements. By 1954 there were nearly five hundred three-bedroomed houses on the estate. There were also forty larger houses, and ninety cottages and flats with one or two bed-rooms suitable for single people, or for married couples whose children had left home.

A Primary School had been built in 1912. A Senior School was built in 1939; and in 1949 a farmhouse owned by the Trust was converted into a small hostel for old people. The original Folk Hall, which had been built in 1906 to serve as a centre for the village's communal activities, was supplemented in 1935 by a new building which had seating accommodation for four hundred and fifty people. Playing-fields and sports grounds were enlarged as cricket and football clubs grew in size and im-portance; and a nursery school was established which children between the ages of two and five could attend in the mornings.

As time went on the older houses were modernized. Bath-rooms were installed in those which had only had a bath in the kitchen with a hinged flap to cover it. The old-fashioned 'York-shire' kitchen ranges, with their open coal fire as the only means of boiling or frying, were replaced by modern heat-storage cookers. Along the roads saplings which had been planted when the first houses were built grew into tall chestnut and sycamore and poplar trees. Grass verges acquired the quality of long-established turf.

In one respect, however, Joseph's ambition remained unfulfilled. For economic reasons it proved impossible, after the first few years, to provide houses within the means of the lowest income-groups. The effort to achieve this object dominated the work of the Trust for the first twenty years of its existence, but it was a struggle against insuperable odds. This became apparent in 1925, by which time all council houses—built for that section of the community with whom Joseph was most concerned—had to be subsidized by the local and central authorities. Today the subsidy amounts to about thirteen shillings a week in most districts.

In other directions, however, Joseph's hopes were fully realized. The village became a real community, and the strength and enthusiasm of the Village Council all through the years bears witness to the interest which the inhabitants took in their domain. As Waddilove says in *One Man's Vision*, New Earswick 'in planning and community organization . . . has contributed much to the conception of a "neighbourhood unit" widely employed today to give a sense of intimacy and cohesion to the new large urban areas now being developed'.

New villages and suburbs may have many amenities, and the houses of which they are composed may have every modern convenience, but they lack the friendly irregularities and the human echoes of old-established settlements. It is not easy to fuse into a whole unconnected families whose roots have been planted in other places, and who may have little in common except the new district to which they have moved. The fact that New Earswick developed into a community with a life of its own is a tribute to the man who realized from the beginning that more than bricks and mortar go to the building of a new village.

CHAPTER FIFTEEN

IN 1905, at the age of thirty-six, Joseph's eldest son died of pneumonia in America, where he had gone to consult a specialist who had once before given him treatment for his failing eyesight.

John Wilhelm and his father had been very close to each other, and Joseph's grief can only be imagined. They had had many things in common. John Wilhelm, as a boy, had worked in his father's business when it was still a small and struggling concern. He could remember, as a child, living in the house which Joseph had furnished for his first marriage. But more important than these links with the past had been Joseph's hopes for the future. John Wilhelm had been a fresh wind blowing through some sections of the Society of Friends. 'The strong individuality of his faith disturbed some members,' says a contemporary account. It had never disturbed his father. Joseph had heard in his son's voice the accent of prophecy, and believed him to be one of those who speak to the people that they may go forward. Now all this was over.

There was another, more trivial, side to Joseph's sorrow. John Wilhelm, like Henry Isaac long ago, could make Joseph laugh; light-heartedness was rare in his surroundings and he prized it. The gaiety and wit which had once endeared John Wilhelm to the men at Tanner's Moat were a very real loss to his father. Indeed, for a great many people, a light was abruptly turned out when John Wilhelm died. To be a man dedicated to God, and at the same time an asset at any social gathering, is an unusual combination.

Joseph was sixty-nine when his eldest son died, and he had begun to think of his own death. There were certain arrangements which he wished to make in good time, particularly about his money.

It is difficult, today, to understand how worried some people could be, fifty years ago, by having too much money. But to men like Joseph it was a great anxiety. These were the days when his income increased yearly, and income tax stood at eightpence in the pound. By taste as well as by conviction the usual wealthy man's ways of spending money were closed to him. To buy a string of race-horses or a yacht or a deer forest would have seemed to him immoral; nor was he interested in such things. He spent money on books, on travel, and on his garden, but these were mild forms of extravagance. He had as little lust for 'things' as John Bright, who long ago had refused to bring back any souvenirs from abroad, saying, 'Our house is full enough of objects'. Nor did Joseph approve of the benevolence which gave thousands of pounds to build hospitals and sanatoriums. In his opinion these things were the responsibility of the State and ought not to depend on private charity. The problem of what to do with his money lay heavily on his mind, for he was afraid of its effect on his family. It was a threat not so much to his children— who had acquired what he describes as 'strenuous habits' early in life—but to his many grandchildren. He wrote a private memorandum and sent copies of it to his sons and daughters. The envelopes were addressed in black ink in his own hand—the beautiful copper-plate with its thick and thin strokes which he had once taught to men in the Adult School. 'The Opportunities and Dangers of Wealth' was the heading.

'We know the typical young fellow,' runs one paragraph, 'full of himself, thinking a great deal about his convenience and his comfort, able to get whatever he wants without effort or self-denial, and who has no high ideal of life . . . when the means are forthcoming it is so easy and so pleasant to give children almost all they ask for, but it is an act of great unkindness on the part of any parent to allow (for want of thought or resolution on their own part) a child to grow up in self-indulgent habits.'

He was an old man but his own childhood was still vivid in his memory. In the house above the Pavement shop there had never been much money, yet the children who were considered so wild by their neighbours had not felt the lack of it. Nor, in spite of a discipline which was very lax by contemporary standards, had they grown up irresponsible. They had been trained, not bullied, into the pattern their parents thought desirable.

It was a pattern that Joseph still followed, and one which he would have liked his descendants at least to consider. 'But', he wrote, 'I know how easy it is, in the various forms of personal expenditure, to acquire step by step expensive habits. One of the mischievous ways in which these habits tell is by increasing the barrier between wealthy people and their fellows. . . . The observation of a life-time has led me to believe that any considerable amount of wealth more often proves to be a curse than a blessing. In the remembrance of this I have, with I believe the hearty assent of my children, given about one-half of my property to the establishment of three Trusts.'

There were, from their beginning in 1904, three separate Trusts. The first was established as a social, charitable, and religious Trust, and its function was to help in financing such things as social surveys, adult education, and the activities of the Society of Friends. The second was also a social Trust in its aims and purposes, but not in its legal form. It had power to undertake social and political work which could not legally be supported by any funds belonging to a charitable trust. In essence these two Trusts had the same purpose, and the distinction between them was regarded by Joseph simply as a legal necessity. The third was the Village Trust, which was concerned with living conditions and in particular with the houses at New Earswick.

Joseph wrote a memorandum for his Trustees. It is not meant, he says, to restrict in any way the full discretion and the free hand which the Trust Deeds deliberately allow them; but it might be helpful for them to know the thoughts which had been in his own mind when he created the Trusts.

It was forty years since Joseph, as a young widower, had spent his evenings in the Pavement counting-house writing an essay on Pauperism, but his ideas about some things had not changed. He had thought then that charity as ordinarily practised, 'the charity of endowment, the charity of emotion', was useless. He thought so still.

'Much of our philanthropic effort is directed to remedying the more superficial manifestations of weakness or evil,' he observes, 'while little thought or effort is directed to search out their underlying causes. . ... It is much easier to obtain funds for the famine-stricken people in India than to originate a searching enquiry into the causes of these recurrent famines. The Soup Kitchen in York never has difficulty in obtaining adequate financial aid, but an enquiry into the extent and causes of poverty would enlist little support. Every social writer knows the supreme importance of questions connected with the holding and taxation of land, but for one person who attempts to master this question there are probably thousands who devote their time to relieving poverty. In my view, therefore, it is highly undesirable that money should be given by the Trusts to Hospitals, Almshouses, or similar institutions.'

The same principle was to be applied to the Society of Friends. Money was not to be given, unless in very special circumstances, towards the building of Meeting Houses, Adult Schools, or Social Clubs. The need for suitable buildings was so obvious that it was certain to be supplied. Nor were the Quaker schools in York to be given money for building alterations, though supplements might be made to teachers' salaries in order to obtain the services of highly qualified men and women. The necessity for these higher salaries, Joseph thought, did not appear to be 'sufficiently seen' by Friends, and the working of supply and demand was not likely to secure an adequate income for the teachers. He adds: 'The need for religious teaching to members of the Society of all ages, is also something which is not clearly seen . . . but upon which a powerful Ministry depends. I would therefore entirely approve of support to the Woodbrooke Settlement, or to kindred efforts.'

The Woodbrooke Settlement had recently been established in a house belonging to George Cadbury, as a Quaker College for advanced Biblical and social studies. It was a project which had grown out of the 'summer schools' run by John Wilhelm.

Joseph's ideas about philanthropy had not altered in forty years, but it is interesting to see how time had changed his attitude towards Church and State. In 1865 they had been the dragons in the path of progress. 'Privilege', then, was still firmly in the saddle. Twenty thousand clergymen were silent when there were wrongs to be righted, and 'only recovered their power of speech when their own order was assailed'.

But in 1904, in Joseph's eyes, the greatest danger to the country was the power of 'selfish and unscrupulous wealth'. It influenced public opinion through the Press, sought only its own ends, and had countenanced the Opium Traffic, the Liquor Trade, and the South African War. If funds permitted, and his Trustees felt equal to the task, he wished them to control a newspaper or newspapers which might divert public thought into more worthy channels.

There are many things in the memorandum which reflect Joseph's years of experience in a widely changing world. He expresses the hope that 'those who come after me will do their best to maintain the purity of *elections* in York'. As a young man he had seen a tradesman sitting in his shop door after a municipal election with a bowl of half-crowns beside him, paying out the coins to those who had given him their vote. And once a man had begged from Joseph on the excuse that the three pounds he had been given for his Parliamentary vote had been stolen.

These days of corruption were ended, and so perhaps was the necessity for protests against slavery, the opium traffic, and intemperance. No man can foresee the future. Joseph knew quite well the limits of his own vision. He says, very simply, 'I hope that nothing I have written may discourage those who will have the administration of these Trusts . . . from entering into fields of service I have not indicated, and which I cannot, at present, foresee'.

Trust Deeds are formal documents, hedged in by the precise language lawyers find necessary. Joseph had to ask his legal advisers to find words which would express his own meaning, and several clauses in the Village Trust are recorded as being inserted at the Founder's special request.

He was anxious that tenants should be associated with the management of the estate, and provision was made for a proportion of representatives from the village to sit with the Trustees at their meetings and to vote on questions which directly concerned them. There was another clause which made possible co-operative ownership of houses by groups of tenants. This scheme has never yet been put into practice at New Earswick. Perhaps it is one of Joseph's ideas with which time has not yet caught up, or perhaps it was simply a safeguard for which there has been no need. 'It is preferable to the property being held by a despotic set of owners, however benevolent,' he observed.

It seems that he did not altogether trust the future, and was a little wary of the developments the years might bring. On the one hand he gave his Trustees the widest possible powers, and on the other he left to the village the possibility of freeing itself from their control.

Joseph hoped that all three Trusts would remain 'living bodies' free to adapt themselves to the changing necessities of the times; and his Trustees have found, in fact, that in the course of fifty-two years there has been little difficulty in interpreting his wishes. His memoranda, which in places seem so simple as to be almost naïve, are a triumphant example of a basic statement of faith and opinion applicable to practically any human situation.

The establishment of the Trusts relieved Joseph of some anxieties about his money. They satisfied his long-held conviction that 'charity', like all other practical matters, ought to be treated scientifically; though it is clear from his account book that he gave away quite large sums of money every year on a most unscientific basis. Apart from the contributions one would have expected—to the Society of Friends, the Adult Schools, the hospital, the Y.M.C.A., the Liberal Association, the Lifeboat Institution, the Band of Hope, and so on—there are many items of a much more personal sort entered as 'Subscriptions, Charity, etc.' in his accounts.

In the days before he was a rich man Joseph made careful notes of all his donations: 'Poor Woman 2/6 . . . Thomas 10/- . . .

Smith to go to London £1 . . . Doughty £2 . . . Bribery prosecution £60.19.3 . . . Gaget's child £2.4.0. . . . Gladstone dinner (difficulty) £1.5.6. . . . S.S. Night nurse for two weeks £2 . . . extra year at Bootham School, C's son £10 . . . Australian voyage of consumptive £10 . . . Stopped gambling at club 15/– . . . T's rent £6.19.6. . . . Education crisis 10/– . . . Education struggle £5.'

I think that many of these entries are deliberately made in a sort of 'shorthand' which only Joseph himself would understand. One would like to know what was the difficulty over the Gladstone dinner, or how it was possible to stop gambling by paying fifteen shillings. Nor is there any clue as to the whereabouts of the crisis and struggle for education. And as time goes on the secrecy grows. 'B.C. £150. T.H. £95.' Finally, in the three years before the Trusts were established, the account book becomes defiantly obscure. 'Sundry small amounts £697. Unaccounted for £196. Sundries £131.' These are the sort of entries he made both on the page dedicated to 'Charity' and the one used to record his own personal 'Sundries'.

It is true that his other accounts are also less detailed than they had been when money was tight, but most of them are still itemized to a certain extent. On the Horse and Carriage page there are still separate statements for hay, rent, shoeing, the coachman's wages and the coachman's clothes; and on another page there are notes as to the amount paid for a morning-room carpet and a bureau.

It seems likely that Joseph, having decided to dispose of half a large fortune in a carefully considered and methodical way, felt free to spend the rest of his money in a more unorthodox fashion. The man who had studied costs all his life, and who still worked out the average price per unit of his newly installed electricity supply, was not likely to set down nearly seven hundred pounds as 'sundry small amounts' without some good reason.

CHAPTER SIXTEEN

JOSEPH, in many ways, followed the domestic pattern
established by his father. In 1858 the elder Joseph had built
the house at the top of St. Mary's for his old age, and had
designed it to be more 'spacious and comfortable' than the rooms
above the Pavement shop or the house in Blossom Street. Now,
in November 1905, Joseph also chose a house for his retirement;
and, like his father, he moved a little farther away from the city.

Clifton Lodge stood on the outskirts of the city. It had
once been a Regency house with a sitting-room on either side
of the front door and a drawing-room and dining-room opening
off the far end of the hall. But the Honourable Reginald Parker,
from whom Joseph bought the house, had made many additions
to it. Much of its symmetry had been lost in a curious haphazard
series of rooms built on to the original structure. Probably, however, this did not trouble Joseph. He had been used to strange
architectural features from his childhood, when the Pavement
house was constantly being altered to accommodate more and
more people.

Several acres of land went with Clifton Lodge, and there were
two cottages attached to it. Joseph had bathrooms installed in
the cottages, and spent a good deal of time rearranging the
gardens. Inside the house the old furniture from St. Mary's was
set in position, some of the carpets were altered and re-laid, and
new curtains were bought. Shelves were built for Joseph's large
library, and his own books and those he had inherited from his
father settled down in a room which, up to now, had been more
used to men whose reading was limited to the *Sporting Times*.

The character of the house changed abruptly when Joseph and
his wife moved into it. No two owners could have been more
different than Joseph and the Honourable Reginald Parker. The
latter had been a man with a passion for horses and hunting, who

had no interest in politics or civic life, and who entertained on the largest possible scale. Joseph continued to live as he had always done, his days occupied with business, his leisure with committees, clubs, children, his garden, his grandchildren, and his books. The particular savour of a Quaker household filled the rooms which had once welcomed house-parties for York races and been decorated with flowers for grand dinners. In the stables, where the hunters had been looked after as carefully as the children in the nursery, there were now only two sedate carriage-horses and Joseph's bicycle. It was, perhaps, a sign of the times.

It was at Clifton Lodge in 1907 that Joseph wrote a pamphlet called 'The First Step', in which he argued that the House of Lords' right to veto Bills sent up to them by the Commons ought to be abolished. Here again his thoughts were turning to the heroes of the past, for it was John Bright who had urged, in 1883, that the Lords should be obliged to pass any Bill sent up to them for the second time. But the day of Privilege was not quite ended. The House of Lords was still powerful, and it was a determined enemy of the Liberal Party. Between 1906 and 1911 the Lords did their best to thwart all the social reforms which the Liberals, backed up by the Irish Nationalists and by the fifty-three Labour members who had now been elected to the Commons, tried to carry out. Bills were either thrown out altogether or passed in a form which made them useless. There was real bitterness between not only Conservatives and Liberals but also between the two Houses of Parliament.

The storm broke in 1909, when Lloyd George introduced what came to be known as the 'People's Budget'.

It had been an established tradition for many years that the House of Lords should pass any Bill dealing with finance. But the 'People's Budget' was too much for them. They rejected it by a large majority, claiming that it was not an ordinary financial measure but a disguised attack upon one particular class—their own. The Commons' retort came two days later. They moved and carried a resolution condemning the House of Lords, and Parliament was dissolved.

In 1909 Edward VII had told the Prime Minister, Mr Asquith, that if *two* general elections made it clear beyond all doubt that the nation was in favour of the Liberal proposals he would consider creating new peers. The King was prepared, in fact, to pack the Upper House with three hundred new titles to ensure that the Lords would pass a Bill which cut the ground from under their own feet.

George V, six months after his father's death, made a similar promise. The Liberal Party prepared a list of those who would be asked to accept peerages if the need arose, and Joseph's name is among them. It is interesting to speculate whether he would have accepted or refused. He did not approve of titles as such. But neither did he approve of the Conservative Party or of the House of Lords. If the only way to abolish the power of a peer was to become a peer, perhaps he would have felt obliged to call himself Lord Rowntree.

The difficult decision, however, did not arise. The only question now before the Upper Chamber was, in Lord Selborne's words: 'Whether we shall perish in the dark, slain by our own hand, or in the light, killed by our enemies.'

The Lords voted for the more dignified death. By a majority of seventeen they passed the Parliament Bill which tied their own hands.

Some time before this Joseph had discovered that he could use his power and his influence in ways more suited to his taste than a seat in the House of Lords could ever have provided. Through the Social Service Trust he had begun to take an interest in journalism.

There had been a great change in the newspaper world in the last two decades of the nineteenth century. It had begun with *Tit-Bits* and *Answers* (in both of which Rowntrees' first advertisements appeared) and had continued with the publication of the *Daily Mail* in 1896, and the *Daily Mirror* in 1904. These were all papers which, unlike their predecessors, cut their Parliamentary reports to the minimum. They were intended for the new reading public which had appeared as a result of the Education

Act of 1870; the people who were not at all interested in speeches made in the House of Commons.

Joseph had grown up in a world where the owner of a newspaper felt a real obligation towards his readers. 'Comment is free but facts are sacred' had been a maxim which was generally accepted. The newspapers which were read aloud at the dinner table in Joseph's youth had had no photographs in them, and few sensational headlines. He had listened to the rolling cadences of the old reporters, and the dignified articles on public affairs which were as carefully composed as essays and as liberally strewn with classical quotations. This was the expensive journalism which could be kept for reference, and quoted authoritatively in discussions. Now it was being challenged by quite a different sort of newspaper; and Joseph, open-minded though he was to changes of every kind, thought this dangerous.

He was alarmed, also, by the decline in the number of provincial newspapers. The new sensational dailies were replacing them by leaps and bounds, 'flooding the country on a tide of imperialistic sentimentality'. He began to wonder whether anti-Liberal and perhaps war-mongering interests might not finally conquer the last strongholds of the English Press.

In the memorandum addressed to his Trustees Joseph had mentioned the possibility of the Social Service Trust controlling a newspaper or newspapers 'if funds permitted and they felt equal to the task'. And very shortly after the Trust was established such an opportunity occurred. The manager of the *Northern Echo* approached Joseph for financial help in starting a York and North Riding edition of the paper.

Joseph made a counter-proposal. He suggested that the Social Service Trust should acquire control over the whole paper, and his suggestion was accepted. This was the beginning of the Trust's interest in newspapers, and it led, in the course of time and by several amalgamations, to the association known as the Westminster Press Provincial Newspapers Ltd., which finally comprised sixteen newspaper companies.

The *Northern Echo* was, naturally, Liberal in its sympathies, but it was by no means narrowly political. It hoped to provide a modest counterblast to the shallow judgements and irresponsible headlines of some sections of the national Press. Rooted though he was in his own city Joseph was never provincial in his thinking, and it was partly through his influence that the *Northern Echo* began to give to matters of national importance some of the attention which had previously been concentrated on parish politics.

Joseph's nephew Arnold was the first chairman of the group of newspapers controlled by the Trust and Mr J. Bowes Morrell was one of the first directors. These two men, both of whom had been on the original board of Rowntree & Co., carried into journalism the practices they had found satisfactory in business. First of all the papers for which they were responsible had to be established on a sound financial basis. They must pay their own way—though it was not necessary that they should show a large profit. *That* could be left to the papers which, in Lord Salisbury's words, were written 'by office boys for office boys'.

A local paper exists to serve its locality, and the *Northern Echo* and its associates never forgot this; but here and there a wind from a different world ruffled the pages. As well as careful lists of wedding guests, or mourners at a funeral, there were leading articles which furnished food for thought. And there were, as in the old days, commentaries on topical subjects which were not afraid to admit that most questions had two sides.

So much for the provinces. And now, cautiously, the Trust began to consider the national Press. It helped to finance *The Nation*, a weekly journal founded by a group of young Liberals in 1907. This paper succeeded *The Speaker* and was itself merged with *The New Statesman* in 1931. The editor was H. W. Massingham, and the chairman of the board of directors was Richard Cross, a solicitor who in his youth had been articled to Joseph's cousin Joshua.

The Nation numbered among its contributors some of the best serious writers of the day, and politicians treated it with respect. Distinguished visitors often added to the liveliness of the weekly staff luncheons, and on these occasions the standard of both wit and of argument was high. The young Liberals who had started the paper were an enterprising group. But here, again, something was missing. The seeds of dissension within the Liberal Party were already sown.

Joseph, who had listened to Gladstone and Disraeli in the days when Whig and Tory were words more commonly used than Liberal and Conservative, may have had misgivings. He had seen the rise of the Liberal Party and he was to see its decline. Not all the brilliance and intelligence surrounding *The Nation* could arrest it.

In December of the year 1905 there was much unemployment in York. Trade was not as good as it had been before the Boer War, and there was vague dissatisfaction in many parts of the country. Prices had risen, and workmen's pay-packets did not go as far as they had done a few years before. On the other hand employers' profits were increasing. The tide which was to lead to strikes in 1910 and 1911 had begun to rise.

Rowntree & Co. remained untroubled by this general discontent. The Firm was growing steadily, and Joseph was able to 'press forward certain building operations which would not in ordinary circumstances have been undertaken for some time'. They were, in fact, started in order to provide work for some of the unemployed in York; and Joseph, as usual, deplored the necessity for such an action. 'It is only a temporary expedient for meeting a pressing difficulty,' he wrote in the *Cocoa Works Magazine*.

He was troubled, as he had been in his youth, by the enormous division between those who were wealthy and those who were not. In these early years of Edward VII's reign the difference showed even more clearly than it had done under Victoria. The Queen's more prosperous subjects had gone in for solid comfort, for clothes and furniture of the very best quality, for enormous meals but no waste in the kitchen. Rich Edwardians permitted themselves more display. Women wore more lace than had been seen for sixty years, and no longer ordered dresses which could be re-trimmed and altered and dyed to last through four or five winters. Food was still copious in quantity, but now it had also become a matter of pride among hostesses to have the first delicacies of the season on their tables regardless of cost. The number of housewives who kept their store-cupboards locked and held inquests on the previous day's left-overs had dwindled. Luxury was no longer a thing of which anyone need be ashamed.

Joseph, though he did not touch even the fringe of the fashionable world, was well aware of the temper of the times. He did not care for it at all. The rich and the poor were still separated by a gap which was very nearly as wide as it had been fifty years before. Ill health and unemployment continued to menace the poor, and in the first years of the twentieth century they were as much of a financial disaster to the working-man as they had been to his grandfather.

As far as industry was concerned illness was a nuisance, and in any business influenced by the Christmas trade it was particularly tiresome. People tended to fall ill at the beginning of the cold weather, just when they were most needed. It was bad for the business and worse for them; for there was no safeguard against sickness until Lloyd George brought in the National Insurance Act of 1911.

Some enterprising firms, however, had begun to employ their own doctors long before the Government scheme was introduced. Cadbury Brothers appointed a doctor for their employees in 1902, and Rowntree & Co. in 1904 did the same.

Peter Macdonald, who had married Joseph's elder daughter, was the Firm's first physician, and those who consulted him at the Works were not required to pay anything for his services. It soon became obvious to him that an enormous proportion of ill-health was due to bad teeth, and he suggested to the directors that a dentist would really be more useful than a doctor at the Works. The directors did not dispense with their doctor, but in 1904 they appointed a dentist as well and the dentist's services were also free.

In Joseph's mind there was no idea of sentimental benevolence about these medical services.

'Healthful conditions of labour are not luxuries to be adopted or dispensed with at will,' he said. 'They are conditions necessary for success. In keen international competition the vigour and intelligence of the workman are likely to be a determining factor.'

Joseph never believed that machines were more important than men, and his foreign investigations on the subject of alcohol had given him, as a side-line, a good deal of other information. American workmen ate more and better food than their English counterparts. The Germans had a better and longer-established educational system. And both these nations, now, were beginning to catch up on the long industrial lead with which Britain had started the nineteenth century.

It seemed clear to Joseph that unless the English workman could be provided with a better diet and a better education Britain would find herself at an increasing disadvantage in the sphere of international trade.

In 1905 a Domestic School was started at Rowntrees. The *Cocoa Works Magazine*, announcing its opening, referred to 'the contention that factory life unfits a girl for home duties by allowing her neither time nor opportunity for learning what is necessary for the management of a home. . . . This has decided the Directors to provide the School and a staff of teachers as a means by which to remedy this defect'.

There was still a trace of benevolent autocracy about Joseph's dealings with his younger employees, and girls who entered the Works before they were seventeen were now obliged to attend the Domestic School's cookery classes. These took up two hours every week, but the girls' time was paid for by the Firm so that unless they were pieceworkers they lost no money by the arrangement. The pieceworkers probably lost a little, for the time they spent in cooking was paid at only the usual rate.

The girls' classes were followed in 1907 by courses for boys in Swedish Physical Training; and a few years later 'continuation classes' were established. These consisted of practical mathematics, English, and woodwork. They also were compulsory

for any boy coming to Rowntrees before his seventeenth birthday, and four hours of the Firm's time were given up to them. In
addition two hours of the boys' own time were demanded of them
in the evenings, and there was occasionally a grievance about this.
Where education was concerned, however, Joseph was not likely
to be moved from the position he had held all his life. He was
sure that in commerce, as in politics and even in religion, the
educated, balanced, lively mind was more necessary than anything else. Enterprising and intelligent workers were as essential
as modern machinery to a firm's success.

In 1906 there were forty men in the Firm described as 'permanent advertising staff'. It was twenty years since Joseph had
allowed the first advertisement to appear, and advertising was
now recognized as one of the most important parts of the business. There were about eighty-five commercial travellers, too, as
compared with the half-dozen who had represented Rowntrees
in the eighties, and they were impressive individuals who still
wore top-hats. Nearly four thousand people were employed
altogether at the Works—two hundred times as many as in 1883.
But some things were still unchanged, and among them was
Joseph's preoccupation with poverty.

Seebohm's book had shown that the unemployed, the old, the
very young, and the sick made up the majority of those in
poverty, and it was with the old that Joseph now concerned
himself. In 1904 he appointed a committee to explore the question
of a Pension Fund.

This was a relatively new idea in the business world, and the
committee took two years to work out how it could best be
arranged. It was, of necessity, very expensive. Seebohm, writing
of its establishment, said, 'Many firms may hesitate to adopt a
Pension Scheme on this account. But it is probable that those
very firms carry a heavy cost in "hidden pensions" without realizing the fact. If a firm establishes a liberal pension scheme it will
doubtless at the same time fix a definite retiring age, and will thus
never find itself with a number of old workers of low working
capacity drawing full pay. . . . Such employees are very costly;

not only does the firm lose on them individually, but their presence tends to lower the pace and lessen the output of the whole
shop. . . . But they are kept on because they have worked faithfully for a great number of years and the management does not
care to dismiss them.'[1]

When Rowntrees' Pension Scheme began to be discussed it
was only thirty-five years since Joseph had first gone to work
with Henry Isaac at Tanner's Moat. Among the three thousand
five hundred and sixty people employed at the Works in 1904
there were several who had been engaged by Joseph during his
early years in the business, and some were not yet old men. A
boy starting work at thirteen, which was the usual age in the
seventies, would be a man nearer forty than fifty at the beginning
of the twentieth century. But even if he had another twenty years
of work left in him he had no chance of saving much against his
old age.

Nowadays most firms make some provision for retirement, but
fifty years ago conditions were very different. When Rowntrees'
Pension Scheme was started State old-age pensions were still two
years away—and when they did come into being they were
modest, even by the standards of the time. They could not be
granted to anyone with a weekly income of more than ten shillings; they could not be claimed until the recipient was seventy;
and the amount was five shillings a week.

Joseph aimed at something better; his hope was to establish
a pension equal to at least half the wage a man was earning when
he retired. Rowntrees' subscription tables were designed to provide minimum pensions of fifteen shillings a week, or one pound
a week if the member's wage was two pounds or more. Employees' contributions varied according to age, the minimum
being two per cent of wages, and the maximum five per cent.
The Company paid into the Pension Fund 30s for every 20s
paid by men, and up to 60s for every 20s paid by women.

From the beginning the Firm accepted the whole responsibility
for the solvency of the Pension Fund, and this was a serious
financial undertaking. A large sum of money was needed to set

[1] Seebohm Rowntree. *The Human Factor in Business.*

it up in the first place, and it was impossible to forecast how much the Company would have to contribute to it in the future. It was *hoped* that in time the cost to the Firm would be no more than two and a half per cent of the total wages and salaries bill, and this was considered reasonable when all the advantages were taken into account. The ultimate cost, in fact, exceeded this figure, though the actual solvency of the Fund was never in doubt after the first few years of its existence.

When the Scheme was started, however, no one could forecast its future. There were few precedents and no certainty of success.

Joseph must have been aware of all the hazards. He was much too good a business man not to have assessed the extent of the financial risk. But the other side of the question carried the day, as far as he was concerned. He found it intolerable that thousands of people should have to make a choice between ending their days in the Workhouse, or living a mean, meagre, poverty-stricken existence all their life in order to make some provision for their old age.

In the early years of the Pension Scheme special concessions had to be made so that men and women who were already at the end of their working life might get reasonable pensions. These were the people who had shared the difficulties of Tanner's Moat with Joseph, the boys and girls he had interviewed long ago, in the office which had a trap-door beside the desk. He was determined now that they too should have some reward.

Joseph gave £10,000 out of his own pocket to the Pension Fund when it was first set up, and the Company gave about £9,000. These were large sums for the time, and they enabled the Scheme to start on a solvent basis, and also to provide for those employees who were due to retire soon after it was established.

Although they had no pattern to guide them, the men who formulated the Pension Scheme at Rowntrees showed uncanny prevision in working out its details. The foundation upon which they built was so basically sound that most of their ideas have survived intact to the present day. They decided, for one thing, that pensions should be on a 'money value' principle, and this meant that although inflationary problems cropped up in later years and the cost of living mounted steadily, pensions could be kept in step with wages.

The investment powers given to the original Trustees of the Pension Fund were very wide. It was unusual, at this time, for any kind of trust to be allowed to invest except in the recognized trustee securities and mortgages; but subject to the written approval of all, or all but one, of their number, the Pension Fund Trustees could invest in '. . . any investment or security in the United Kingdom'. Some years later this clause was modified to include investment in properties, and the stipulation about the written approval of the Trustees was abolished. Otherwise the Trustees' powers are substantially the same today as they were fifty-one years ago.

Nor, on the benefit side, has the original Scheme required much modification, though benefits today are very much greater and pensions can now be subscribed for sums which (together with allowance for State benefit) amount to two-thirds of wages. However the arrangements for the appointment of Trustees and the general management of the Fund have remained practically unaltered for half a century.

There is no doubt that Joseph and his fellow-directors filled an enormous need by setting up their Pension Scheme in 1906, and this was proved by ninety-eight per cent of those employees who were eligible joining it in that year.

Eleven years later, during the First World War, another need became apparent. Many of the widows of men who had died on active service were in great financial difficulties. The Company had started a fund in 1911 to increase to a minimum of £50 the money payable to a widow when her husband died, and later this amount had been raised to £100. But Joseph felt that this was quite inadequate. He pressed for the establishment of a Widows' Benefit Fund, which, under certain conditions, would provide pensions for widows who were aged fifty or more at the time of their husband's death. (The qualifying age later became forty-five.)

At a Board Meeting in 1917 he made a memorable request:

'I am so much impressed with the need and value to our people of the proposed arrangement,' he said, 'that I ask the Board to accept the principle before discussing the cost.'

He could have said nothing which would have made a deeper impression on his fellow-directors. All through his business career he had been noted for his careful analysis of costs. Costing had been his first work at Tanner's Moat, and he had never lost sight of its importance. The Board realized that his request was a departure from the habit of a lifetime, and saw how much the new Fund meant to him. It was started almost at once.

Manufacturing finally stopped at Tanner's Moat in 1908. This year saw the very end of the inconvenient workrooms, the long flights of stairs, and all the awkward makeshifts which had been the nursery of the Firm's prosperity. But even before Tanner's Moat ceased to be part of the Works another and much more important change had occurred. The old ideal of paternalism had finally died.

For many years at Tanner's Moat, Joseph had maintained an authoritative and responsible attitude towards his employees. He was the 'master' of his business in the medieval sense. His workmen were given such things as he considered it proper for them to have. The decisions were all his own.

Even the best employers did not get much further than this at the end of the nineteenth century; but now the ferment of the twentieth century was at work, and Joseph's ear was close to the ground. 'Time makes ancient good uncouth' was one of his pet quotations; and by 1907 his attitude towards his employees had changed a good deal.

'I have no doubt', he wrote in a private memorandum, 'that as the intelligence and self-control of the workers increase, claims will be made for the share of profit which comes to Labour to be augmented, while the share which comes to Capital is lessened. Now the temptation to the Directors of the Cocoa Works, both in their position as Directors and as well-to-do politicians, will be to take a merely Capitalistic view of these demands. . . . I believe we have been right so far, in creating a Pension Fund and establishing a minimum rate of wages. But what I wish to urge is that these *are only the first steps*. Whether in the future any profit-sharing scheme, or anything in the nature of a co-operative scheme, should be entered upon I cannot say. But I hope that those upon whom the Direction of the Company rests will be prepared, as new problems present themselves, to deal with them with large-hearted and unselfish intelligence.'

Profit-sharing, in 1907, was not altogether a new idea. One authority traces it back to a French house-decorator in 1840, another to an American glass-manufacturer in 1794. In a book called *Thrift* written by Samuel Smiles and published in 1875, three English profit-sharing schemes are described. Joseph, who read Smiles with a critical eye, gave a good deal of thought to these early experiments. Two of them were abandoned quite quickly. Was it a coincidence that these 'promising partnerships' were dissolved in firms which already had a long history of strikes and quarrels over wages, and where profit-sharing was made conditional upon the men *not* joining any trade union? Samuel Smiles blamed the workmen in both cases. They had been too stupid to see the advantages of the scheme, and insisted on re-joining their unions and pressing for higher wages which they did not always get.

The third profit-sharing arrangement described by Mr Smiles was started by the carpet-making firm of John Crossley & Sons. They had been noted for more than one generation for their just and generous dealing with their employees. Martha Crossley, wife of the firm's founder, had worked at a loom her-self, and for years played an active part in the factory. She was shrewd and hard-headed, but she looked at any situation as much from the worker's as the owner's point of view. She urged her sons to arrange matters, if it was at all possible, so that they need not dismiss anyone in winter, 'for it is a bad thing when a man has to go home and hear his children cry from cold as well as hunger'. And when the Crossley fortunes improved, and they moved to new and larger premises, Martha Crossley, going down to the mill yard at four o'clock one morning, made a vow. 'If the Lord do bless us in this place the poor shall taste of it!' The thought behind that pledge had nothing to do with charity. It was her intention that the workpeople should have a share in any success the firm might have—unconditionally. When profit-sharing was introduced in this business, half a century later, it was a logical development of an old-established policy. It was also completely satisfactory and successful. No doubt when he read this Joseph drew his own conclusions.

The whole question, however, was a difficult one, and it was made more complicated by the introduction of the word 'co-partnership'. This term, which was very differently interpreted by different people, often aroused both fear and anger. It was intolerable, to many managers, that their workers should dream of any measure of control in the firm which employed them, either by acquiring share capital, or by setting up committees of workers who would have a voice in the internal management of the factory. Nor was it often suggested that the worker *was* in fact a partner by virtue of the labour he contributed to any undertaking, and that real 'co-partnership' meant the recognition and acknowledgement of this in specific ways—of which profit-sharing was usually one. Such ideas were not popular in most quarters, and many employees regarded them with suspicion as only another expression of the paternalism from which they were trying to escape. The Trade Unions were unanimously hostile, and Beatrice and Sidney Webb described profit-sharing as a 'disastrous undermining of the solidarity of the whole working class'.

Among Joseph's co-directors there was no enthusiasm for a profit-sharing scheme when he first mentioned it in 1907, and it was nine years before the subject was raised again. But he did not lose sight of something which he clearly regarded as a desirable part of a new industrial order. He was a man who knew when it was essential to wait.

CHAPTER SEVENTEEN

JOSEPH did not make enemies. Shrewd though he was in business his success left no unpleasant aftertaste. As a business man as well as a private individual, he was generally regarded with affection as well as respect. There came a time, however, when the new connection between the Rowntree Trust and the Press aroused a certain amount of hostile criticism.

The Trust's position, in this instance, was not unique. George Cadbury, when he bought the *Daily News*, had been the object of several attacks as silly as they were venomous; and it was about this time that the contemptuous phrase 'the Cocoa Press' was first used in an article in *The World*.

In 1907, in the House of Commons, Bonar Law said: 'I think it is very unreasonable and most unfair that the large fortunes which are made in this country out of the cocoa industries should be used, as they are, to subsidize newspapers and to finance members of parliament whose influence is used to prevent other people getting the same advantages as they themselves enjoy.'

It was a muddled speech and a piece of muddled thinking, and there was more bitterness behind it than can be accounted for by the subject upon which it was pinned—the tax differentiation between raw and manufactured cocoa.

It was this world of mud-slinging and acrimonious pin-pricks which the Rowntree Trust entered in 1910, when they acquired, with Cadbury's, an interest in the *Morning Leader* and the *Star*. These were two London newspapers which the Conservative Party would have liked to control, and they were not pleased by the change of ownership. The Conservative papers launched a furious campaign against Cadburys and Rowntrees; accusing them, among many other things, of 'organized cant and hypocrisy'.

The *Star* was a great betting paper, and it did not give up its betting news. 'Old Joe' and 'Captain Coe', tipsters with an enormous following, went on giving their naps and doubles as they had always done. Criticism of this came quickly both from within the Society of Friends and from many other quarters.

Some of the attacks were ill-informed and malicious, but no one could deny the incongruous fact that a body of men whose views on the immorality of gambling were well known were helping to publish newspapers which gave daily advice on the best horses to back. A pamphlet written by Sir Edward Fry, and addressed to members of the Society of Friends, says flatly that 'the National Anti-Gambling League is largely supported by members of the Rowntree and Cadbury families; these very men who are themselves among the principal owners of the Sporting Press'.

Yet the situation was not quite as simple as it may seem. 'The Friends Against Whom Sir Edward Fry's Criticisms have been Directed,' stated their case in a pamphlet of their own.

'We were led to accept this responsibility', they say, 'because we viewed with great anxiety the daily Press of the country passing more and more into the hands of those whose avowed policy and ultimate aims we believe to be an imminent peril to the State. . . . Our position will be understood if we examine the particular case of the *Star*, which exercises great political influence. The *Star* has always supported campaigns for social reform, has helped to expose the evils of Sweated Industries, the Opium Traffic, and the Congo Horrors, and has consistently raised its voice on the side of peace and the reduction of armaments. . . .

'When we were asked to undertake responsibility for the *Star* we put off our decision for a considerable time, and meanwhile urged those who were pressing the paper upon us to make renewed efforts in other directions. They made these efforts but failed. When they came to us again for a final answer the question before us was whether it was right to accept responsibility for the paper, even though it contained features of which we gravely disapproved, or to allow it to pass into the hands of those who would have reversed its policy on many questions.

'Let it be noted that it was *not* in our power to escape the responsibility. If we came to the assistance of the paper it could be saved; otherwise it must pass into hostile hands. . . . There are not so many daily newspapers willing to take the unpopular side, and to make a brave fight for national righteousness even to the extent of opposing the leaders of their own political party, that the country can lightly dispense with one of them.'

It cannot have been an easy decision either for George Cadbury or for the Rowntree Trust. They must have known that they would be laying themselves open to severe criticism. And it was unfortunately a fact that no halfpenny or penny newspaper could survive if it ignored the racing results. George Cadbury had proved this for himself. His first venture into journalism, the long-established *Echo*, had failed six months after he bought it and suppressed the betting page.

'That Sir Edward Fry should deprecate and condemn our decision gives us no ground for surprise or complaint,' the pamphlet continues, 'but we hardly expected that he would describe us, by innuendo, as taking the devil into partnership to aid the Almighty.'

Both protagonists then descend into an argument of the 'You're another' sort, which does not do much to clarify the issue and is perhaps better forgotten. The judgement of a later generation would probably uphold those who set the value of a free Press above the desirability of suppressing the tipsters.

'I sought to be guided by common sense,' George Cadbury said, 'and it seemed evident that the *Star* with betting news and pleading for peace and social reform was better than the *Star* (still with betting news) opposing social reform and stirring up strife.'

Nevertheless unkind things continued to be said, and as the *Manchester Guardian* remarked: 'The Cadburys and the Rowntrees are assailed with such severity and with tones of such severe morality, that a careless reader of the controversy might have supposed that they had introduced a gambling newspaper for the first time into the white-robed company of the London daily Press.'

There seems to be a disproportionate amount of anger underlying the whole affair of the betting news, but perhaps it can be
accounted for by the increasing power which was now seen to
lie in the hands of families like the Cadburys and the Rowntrees.
With their marked success in business, their influence over
thousands of employees, their interest in every kind of reform,
and their indifference to public honours or social rewards, they
were, in some quarters, regarded as a dangerous nuisance. There
was no knowing what untidy part of England they might not
wish to investigate next, and it was clear that they were not to be
easily diverted. A certain section of the population regarded them
as a definite menace, and heartily wished they would stay where
they belonged, making money and spending it as wealthy men
should. There would have been no criticism if they had bought
great country estates or collected pictures, but it was outrageous
that they should be able to buy newspapers, refuse to toe a party
line, and conduct intelligent investigations into matters which
some people would have preferred to ignore.

Perhaps it was this feeling that so much power and independence of spirit were a dangerous combination which made certain
sections of the Press fall with enthusiasm upon an episode known
in its day as the 'Cocoa Scandal'.

Rowntrees were not, in fact, purchasers of cocoa from the
Portuguese islands of San Thomé and Principe, but with three
other firms—of whom Cadburys were one—they shared in the
cost of an investigation into the methods of recruiting native
workpeople. The results of this investigation showed that
W. H. Nevinson's book *A Modern Slavery* had not exaggerated
conditions on the islands. After many unavailing efforts to per-
suade the Portuguese Government to take action the English
firms came to the conclusion that the only course open to them
was to stop trading with San Thomé and Principe. The end of
the story—which involved a sensational libel action—does not
concern Rowntrees, but the publicity surrounding the affair did
in the end do the slaves some useful service. The Portuguese
Government eventually remodelled the system of contracted
labour, and Mr Burtt, the original investigator, saw the return to

their native land of the first men and women ever to be re-patriated.

From the controversies of the larger world it is pleasant to return to the city of York, which, in May 1911, bestowed on Joseph the highest honour within its power. He was made an Honorary Freeman of the City.

York was not prolific in bestowing this award. From 1746 to 1911 only twenty-three names appear upon the Honorary Free-man's Roll, and of these seven are princes of English royal blood. The others are generals and admirals, dignitaries of the Church, a couple of eminent barristers, and some peers of the realm. Joseph was the first man of business to repeat the strange old words of the oath; and to make it by affirmation, as was the Quaker practice.

The Very Reverend Dean Purey-Cust was made a Freeman on the same day, and referred in his speech to his content-ment at being 'a municipal twin of Mr Rowntree's on this occasion'.

Did they remember, these two old men, that the Quaker George Fox had once been thrown out of York Minster and down the steps? Was Joseph amused to find himself bracketed with a member of that Church against which, in his youth, he had written such bitter tirades? He had been obliged, in his own words, to 'submit to a top-hat' and his face wears a mildly quiz-zical expression. But dignity was the order of the day. In his reply to the Lord Mayor's speech Joseph paid tribute to the 'honoured and beloved' Dean of York, and Dr Purey-Cust's oration ended with compliments to one who had done 'so much to promote the commercial prosperity of the city, and whose efforts to advance the welfare of all classes are recognized and appreciated by us all'.

The Mayor and Council, splendid in their robes, made their speeches of welcome to these two respected citizens, recalling Dr Purey-Cust's work for the York County Hospital, for the Musical Society, and for the fabric of the Minster itself; reviewing Joseph's achievements at the Cocoa Works, the establishment of the model village of New Earswick, and the many 'generous and often unrecognized' contributions which he had made to the life of the city.

Joseph's was the final speech of the day, and he began by surveying the growth of York as he had known it in his lifetime, mentioning the improvement in public health, the building of new schools, the establishment of a Free Library and the reform of municipal elections. He dipped far into the past to tell his audience of a time when the little river Foss had been an open drain running through the city, and as a boy he had hurried across it holding his nose to avoid the stench from the water. He spoke of days when one man in three could not sign his name, and even the most upright did not hesitate to accept money for their vote in a Parliamentary election. With affectionate pride and statistical details he remembered how these things had been changed, and told of all that the city had done to provide the essentials of life for its inhabitants.

Then, curiously, and at the very end of his speech, he paints a dark picture which stands out too vividly for comfort among the polite phrases and graceful compliments which had set the tone of that pleasant afternoon.

'But if we make a true survey of the life of our city we know there is another side to it. Which of us has not known cases such as this, bewildering in their difficulty and in the impossibility of offering any satisfactory solution? The breadwinner in the family breaks down in health; his wages cease; with illness the family expenses increase. The payments of the sick club come to an end. The rent falls behindhand; the neighbouring shop, which has given some credit, refuses to increase it. The children, too young to earn wage, are insufficiently fed; the over-taxed mother is in danger of breaking down; the landlord, who has given reasonable credit, cannot extend it, and says that the family must leave at an early date. The only asset is the furniture, purchased by difficult saving before marriage. If brought under the hammer it will realize much less than was given for it, and the family will be left destitute. In despair the mother appeals to one with the question, "What shall I do?"

'A gift may relieve the momentary distress but in giving it we feel the inadequacy, almost the heartlessness, of any counsel we can offer.

'Sometimes, in other cases, the breadwinner dies before the children are able to bring any wage; or the man himself is less bright than his fellows, and in times of dull trade is the first to be dismissed. Or, if skilful, failure of eyesight may destroy his market value. Or, again, changes in the process of manufacture may render valueless a skill laboriously acquired. Or a change of fashion, or a general dullness of trade, may suddenly swell the ranks of the unemployed.

'What street is there in the working-class districts of this city in which one or other of these tragedies is not known? We are apt to comfort ourselves with the thought that the sterner virtues are developed in association with poverty. But poverty is one thing—and destitution is another.'

It was a challenge to a company of prosperous citizens, to the men in their gowns of office, and the women in their garden-party dresses and big elaborate hats. A nasty detailed account of misery around the corner obtruded for a moment into the agreeable and picturesque proceedings in the Guildhall.

The reporters closed their notebooks, the ladies' skirts rustled, and everyone moved into the state dining-room of the Mansion House for tea. But the shadow of reality, the echo of despair from mean streets and sordid houses, went with them. The unfamiliar grandness of the occasion had stirred in Joseph that questioning and protesting spirit which had never long been quiet since he went as a boy to Ireland in the years of the famine. For his own city and his own time he had provided answers to some of the points he raised; but most of the questions which he asked that afternoon were only generally accepted as valid and demanding of a solution with the publication of the Beveridge Report in 1942 and the social legislation which followed the Second World War.

CHAPTER EIGHTEEN

IN the years between 1911 and 1925 Joseph remained out-
wardly much as he had always been: shrewd, calm, remarkably vigorous in body, and as open-minded as any young
man. He was going deaf, but at seventy-five he still went up a
flight of stairs two at a time, and was prepared to give dispassionate consideration to any new idea from any quarter.
There was no trace of defeat in his face. Yet once, speaking of
Thomas Hardy's novels, he said: 'I can't read them. They're
poison to a pessimist like myself.'

It is a puzzling and unexpected remark, since no one ever suspected him of looking on the dark side of things, and his composure in all circumstances had become proverbial. But a streak
of melancholy ran in this branch of the family. Joseph's father
had had to fight against it, and his son John Wilhelm described
to a friend how at one period of his life a cloud of gloom settled
over him regularly at midday and did not lift until between five
and six in the evening. Probably Joseph himself had not altogether escaped this family tendency towards depression.

And now, in these years just before the First World War, a good
many things were happening which dismayed even the most
optimistic.

The date 1914 has a ring of fire around it. The very figures
seem symbols of doom and disaster, dividing a happy sunlit
summer from the mud and misery of the trenches. The shadow
of the war makes the years which led up to it look by contrast
tranquil and light-hearted; years when trade was good and
money was spent lavishly; when garden-parties and balls made
London gay in summer, and hunting and shooting parties filled
country houses in the winter. The clinking of tea-cups in pleasant
gardens, the rustle of skirts at a ball, all the well-ordered elaborate
routine of life in Edwardian England has a romantic glow about

it because of what came later. But there was another, very different, side to the story.

In 1911, a month after Joseph had been made a Freeman of the
city of York, he had not far to look beyond its boundaries to see
a disquieting picture. In Goole and in Hull the seamen and the
dockers were on strike. Rioting crowds threatened to set the
docks on fire. A Hull town-councillor, who had known Paris
during the Commune of 1871, said that things there had been no
worse; he had never realized that there were such people in
England as the half-nude women with streaming hair who reeled
through the streets smashing and destroying whatever they could
lay hands on.

There were similar stories from other parts of England: from
cotton-mills in Lancashire, from coalmines in Wales, from the
docks at Southampton, and from the transport workers in Manchester. Even in the confectionery trade there were strikes. The
women workers in a large sweet factory in Bermondsey left their
work in mid-morning. They went singing and shouting through
the streets, and from other workshops and factories more women
poured out to join them. The stifling air was filled with the
smell of boiling sugar and hot bodies, and it echoed with a
demand for higher wages.

Fear lay over the country. Almost every regiment in England
was kept ready for action. Apart from the strikes, the international situation was dangerous in the extreme. There was the
Agadir crisis and there was trouble in Ireland.

The problem of Ireland had always been of great interest to
Joseph, and politics had never lost their hold over him. The
world of industry was his world. And now, through the Irish
countryside, through the Parliamentary debates, through factories and workshops all over England, there breathed the spirit
of violence which by nature and training and experience he
dreaded more than anything else. It was a disillusioning time
for a man whose imagination was still active, and whose memories went back to more hopeful years.

But however badly things were going in some places the Cocoa

Works had no staff troubles at this period. In the *Cocoa Works Magazine* for these years there is no hint of friction or discontent. The Cricket Club had two record seasons, the building of a new Dining Block was started, the boys in the firm made increasing use of the library, and *The Deerslayer* and *The Fifth Form at St. Dominic's* were the two books in greatest demand. Joseph's domain seems to have been unmoved by the turbulence which stirred so many parts of the country.

In New Earswick, too, everything was going smoothly. More houses were built in the village each year, and although the financial margin was narrow, it was still possible to achieve the Trust's original object and provide good cottages within the means of low-paid workers. A Folk Hall had been built and a Football Club started. The Village Council was finding its feet, and beginning to agitate about the schooling of its children.

This was a project into which Joseph could enter with all his heart. In a world where so much was changing one thing stood unquestioned: the need for better education. Moreover he could spend money on it with a clear conscience. It was not an experiment like the village itself, which must pay a reasonable return on the capital invested if it was to serve as a model for other schemes. The school could be considered as something quite independent of the village, and there was no obligation to cut the cost of it down to the lowest possible point.

The County Education Authority, after some years' delay, classified New Earswick school as 'non-provided'; which meant that although the building had been put up by private effort provision for the education within its walls became the responsibility of the local authority. It was an arrangement often made where Church Schools were concerned, but the New Earswick school, in its charter, specifically excluded instruction distinctive of any particular religious body.

There was another slightly unusual feature about the New Earswick educational system. The managers, four of whom were appointed by the Trustees and two by the Education Authority, were unwilling to allow any one class to hold more than thirty children. In the York area classes of fifty to sixty were common, and the local authorities could obviously not be expected to make special arrangements for New Earswick. Consequently the Trustees appointed and paid for a teacher of their own. Later, as the school grew, they increased the number to three.

Joseph had always valued good teaching above good buildings, but when the Trust established the school at New Earswick they set an architectural standard which was to be unsurpassed for many years. In 1913 the idea of classrooms which had one wall filled entirely by a window was revolutionary. There are schools still in use which are not much older than the one at New Earswick, and their high narrow windows and gloomy passages show how novel the Trust's design must have seemed at the time. The old idea that a child's attention would be distracted if it could see out of a window still existed when the school in which Joseph took so great an interest was built; but the New Earswick children had windows reaching to the ground in all their rooms which in fine weather could be opened back completely. They also had adequate cloakrooms and an unparalleled amount of space between their desks. Joseph and his Trustees, in these matters, anticipated the requirements of the Education Authority by thirty years. When new regulations came into force in 1944 no changes were found to be necessary at New Earswick except for some rearrangement of the electric lights.

One thing is recorded as being Joseph's particular contribution to the educational amenities of New Earswick. In 1915 he was worried because too many children were leaving school too early, and he was sure that the one annual scholarship to a grammar school which was then given was not enough. There must surely be more than one child every year who would benefit by a secondary education? He took his anxieties to the Trust, and it was arranged, finally, to award as many or as few scholarships as there were suitable applicants. The head mistress of a local grammar school was appointed to judge the children's examinations, and their school records at New Earswick were taken into consideration as well.

The Trust paid the grammar school fees of those children who were successful in the examination, gave a grant for buying books, and, where necessary, a maintenance allowance to their parents. By this means one hundred and eighty-five children achieved a secondary education where only twenty-eight could have done so in the ordinary way. If any proof is needed of the value of this education it can be supplied from the records. A third of the children who were helped through the grammar schools later qualified for some profession. It was a notable achievement at a time when only a very small percentage of elementary school children went on to grammar schools at all.

With the new Education Act of 1944 the Trust's private arrangements ended. It was no longer possible to pay for children to attend a grammar school; and, theoretically at least, all those who were likely to benefit by an academic education were now to have it provided by the State. But the experiment had proved, once again, the value of independent enterprise in paving the way for statutory authorities. Perhaps Joseph, as the grim war years went on, drew a little comfort from the fact that he had helped to equip some of the younger generation with the knowledge which was to be so much needed in the future.

The position of a pacifist was not easy in the First World War. Feelings ran high, and even those men who were beyond military age did not always escape harsh criticism. Nevertheless Arnold Rowntree, member of Parliament for York since 1910, was not allowed by his constituents to resign, though he had offered to do so on account of his uncompromising adherence to the Quaker Peace Testimony. Probably very few citizens of York shared his views, but they liked and respected the man himself too much to let him go.

Joseph was seventy-five when war broke out, but he faced new situations, still, with the resilience of a much younger man. Steadily he continued to do what had to be done, though he must have watched with sorrow the destruction of many of his hopes. He had been a worker for peace all his life. Nor did he escape more personal grief. In 1915 his younger daughter died a week after the birth of her third child; and in 1917 one of his grandsons was killed in action. He was twenty-two, and the only son of John Wilhelm.

Yet life goes on, even in the middle of war. It was still possible to go abroad until 1915, and Joseph had one winter holiday in the South of France while fighting was going on in the North. Nor did the war interfere very greatly with manufacturing at the Cocoa Works. Young men went away to fight, and week after week, month after month, their pictures in the *Cocoa Works Magazine* tell of their deaths. The new Dining Block served as a temporary barracks for troops, and later was used as a hospital; and Belgian refugees were billeted in some of the New Earswick houses.

Not many men in their seventies have the fire of youth. But Joseph, at the end of his life, still possessed the well-tempered enthusiasm and the intellectual curiosity which had been characteristic of him as a young man. He spoke deliberately and sometimes slowly; but he never left an idea alone until he had sucked it dry. And now, from the long harvest of his business years, from the theories expounded by the giants of his youth, from much reading and even more from his own experience, he had reached certain very definite conclusions.

They were, as might have been expected, eminently practical. First of all there must be a measure of trust between employers and employed. This had always been the foundation of any good business, but when factories were small it had not been hard to achieve. In the mid-morning break, over cups of tea in the afternoon, the heads of different departments had been able in three sentences to find out the reasons behind any change of plan. They, in turn, could pass on to the men and women working for them explanations unclouded by any intermediate interpreter.

'Mr. Joseph thinks we should do so-and-so——'

'Mr. Seebohm wants to try such-and-such——'

Once long ago it had been informal and unconsidered. Now it was not. Between the girls in their white overalls and the men in their offices there was an inevitable chain of forewomen, foremen, heads of departments, and technical experts. And yet, somehow, the gap had to be bridged.

Mary Follett, an American expert on industrial psychology, found when she visited Rowntrees that the Firm had a habit which she considered rare and strange. Once a year, immediately after the Chairman of the Board had given the usual address to the shareholders, another meeting was held. It was open to all the employees, and questions were invited. A complete survey of the year's work—a good deal more comprehensive than the one laid before the shareholders—was given to those who had been the means of achieving it. They were, without undue emphasis, pledged to secrecy regarding the information thus put in their hands. And without exception they honoured the trust. Not from any of the employees, young or old, who attended these meetings, did anything which occurred at them ever become public property.

There were other arrangements in the factory which were designed to lessen the distance between those who directed the Firm's policy and those who carried it out. 'Works Councils' were established, each consisting of broadly equal numbers of administrative staff appointed by the management, and workers elected by ballot among themselves. The first of these councils was set up during the war, a year before the Whitley Government Committee recommended the same system to industry in general. They were at first regarded with suspicion by the Trade Unions, who thought their own authority might be undermined, but in practice it was found that the Unions' power was not, in fact, weakened by the councils; and shop stewards became an integral part of the new arrangements. These shop stewards were members of Trade Unions, and it was their job to speak for the workers in any matter arising between them and the management. In Factory Departmental Councils the shop stewards *ex-officio* represented the section in which they worked.

All this sounds a little cumbrous, and perhaps time was sometimes wasted while councils debated and shop stewards talked long-windedly. But at least no one was kept in the dark about what was going on in the factory. Doubts could be voiced and questions answered.

The years of the First World War and the period which followed it were critical and difficult in most industries. At this moment, when working conditions were better for most people than they had ever been before, there was more discontent and suspicion than there had been for years. Labour was up in arms. It suspected that even the best employers thought, finally, only of their own advantage. Profit-sharing schemes, joint consultative councils, all the best welfare arrangements, were seen by many workers as a sop to their own growing power, and an indirect method of getting higher profits in which they themselves would not share.

Fear has long memories. The men who distrusted their employers in the twenties remembered their fathers' struggle to get a living wage and a working day of reasonable length. Confidence is not a thing which can be built up overnight, and it can never be achieved at all unless people are told the truth and told it quickly. There are plenty of modern examples of lack of confidence lying at the bottom of a strike.

Perhaps not all strikes are avoidable, even under the most skilled and imaginative management, but in the whole history of Rowntrees—apart from the General Strike of 1926—there have been only two others. Both these were of minor character and short duration, and even in the General Strike those who were 'out' asked to be given an opportunity to return to work long before it ended.

Joseph was now an old man, but his mind kept pace with the twentieth century. The great factory of which he was head moved steadily and consistently forward, with a clear-cut policy behind its progress. More and more responsibility rested on the employees. The Works Councils were asked to help in a revision of the 'Works Rules', which had been drawn up long ago and entirely without consultations with the employees of the time. A vote was taken in 1919 from everyone on the rearrangement of hours, with the result that longer time was worked in the working week and the factory closed all day on Saturday. This was a very popular change. Popular, too, was the decision to grant all factory workers a week's holiday with pay every year. This was done in 1918, at a time when such a practice was still very unusual, and nineteen years before a Bill enforcing 'holidays with pay' came before Parliament. But perhaps the most significant change of all was the decision to give each workroom a voice in the appointment of its foreman or forewoman.

This last arrangement was made in 1923, nearly thirty years after the October morning when a handwritten 'manifesto' had waited on Joseph's desk at Tanner's Moat asking for the removal of the foreman in charge of a certain department. Perhaps he remembered, as some of his fellow-directors wondered doubtfully whether the workers would seek popular easy-going people to govern them, that the long-ago protest had been against inefficiency, not against strictness. Experience, in fact, proved that the workrooms' judgement was sound. A small committee from each department was asked to give their opinion on the individual nominated by the management. If they approved of the appointment the matter was settled. If they disapproved it was their turn to suggest someone else, and his or her appointment was then discussed by a joint committee of management and workers. The directors reserved the right to have the final word if no agreement could be reached, but fifteen years after the scheme's inception Seebohm Rowntree recorded that they had never needed to exercise that right.

It was, perhaps, a roundabout way of filling a post. The usual practice in industry was for the management to select foremen chiefly on their capacity to 'get the most out of those in their department'. But there is more than one way to interpret that phrase, and probably Rowntrees, in the long run, saved time and trouble by a method which was considered very strange by their more arbitrary contemporaries, though it had been tried in at least one trade before the First World War. The spindle-makers in Yorkshire had early acquired the right to choose their own foremen, who controlled the discipline of the workshops, and no single case of trouble was reported either by management or men while this system was in force.

The spindle-makers, however, were a rare exception to the

general rule of their time, and it is still very unusual today to find a factory in which the workers are consulted when their immediate superiors are appointed.

'Yet I think it would be true to say', Seebohm Rowntree wrote of his own firm in 1938, 'that neither party feels that any mistakes have been made in these appointments . . . since the original arrangement was made.'

The procedure at Rowntrees has now been modified. Today the management makes the nomination, but consults the appropriate shop steward before an appointment is made.

It is difficult, in these last years of Joseph's working life, to discover how many of the new ideas in the factory originated with him and how many were due to his son Seebohm. Seebohm, who would obviously become the next managing director of the Firm when his father retired, was already taking much of the responsibility in matters of policy. It is noticeable, however, that almost all the most significant moves towards democratic government within the business were made while Joseph was still at the head of it. Although many of the inspirations may have been Seebohm's he could hardly have put them into practice without his father's concurrence; and one instance is recorded of a project which might have been postponed for a long time had it not been for Joseph's quiet insistence.

It was in 1916 that he began once more to talk about profit-sharing, and found his directors no more enthusiastic about it than they had been nine years before. Their attitude was not surprising. There had been a Board of Trade report on profit-sharing schemes in 1912, which showed that fifty-five per cent of them had been 'abandoned', and that the average life of such schemes was only five years. But calmly and obstinately Joseph persisted. What did 'abandoned' mean? *Why* had the schemes failed? He wrote a memorandum in which he said, 'I believe those who have given thought to the subject hold that a profit-sharing scheme is not applicable to a business like ours. This may be so, and I do not see my way out of the difficulties. But if no form of collective profit-sharing is possible *how* can we secure that an intelligent interest in the prosperity of the business shall permeate through the entire body of workers?'

He listened to all the arguments and to the protest of labour that profit-sharing was an attempt to weaken the power of Trade Unions by individual bargaining between single firms and their employees. He heard people say that workmen always lived up to every penny of their income, and if their share of profits did not materialize in a bad year they would find themselves in debt; and he heard, also, of two different firms who had run a profit-sharing scheme since 1866, and had no doubt of its success.

It was time, once more, for statistics. Joseph and Seebohm who, though doubtful at this time, was open-minded, set an enquiry on foot. William Wallace, who had recently joined the company and later became its Chairman, was asked to make an investigation. The results of his report were curious, and show how misleading even Board of Trade reports can be. He discovered, among other things, that of the 183 schemes which had been 'abandoned' more than fifty per cent had failed because of circumstances which had nothing to do with profit-sharing. In some cases the war, or the fact that there *were* no profits, had put an end to the experiment. In other cases the death of the head of the firm, or a change of management, had stopped the scheme.

Mr Wallace finally reached the conclusion that sixty-six per cent of profit-sharing schemes had been, in fact, successful; and that a number of the rest had failed because they had been introduced from the wrong motives, or because there were defects in the composition of the scheme itself.

The investigation confirmed what Joseph had probably suspected when he read Samuel Smiles. If profit-sharing was used as a weapon against Trade Unionism, which was the frankly expressed reason for a good many nineteenth-century employers introducing it, it was not likely to be successful. Nor, as the twentieth century found, was it a good way of getting better production quickly. People are seldom spurred to great daily efforts by a reward they will not see for a year or eighteen months. Profit-sharing was, in fact, no universal panacea. In factories where a good relationship between employers and employed was lacking it did little to improve the situation. 'Just a racket to make us work harder' was a common verdict from bench and workroom. Only when a company had already gained the confidence of its employees was profit-sharing seen as a genuine attempt by those at the top of the firm to give those at the bottom a share in its success.

In favourable circumstances, however, the advantages of profit-sharing seemed, in fact, to go far beyond the financial aspect. The money any man received in a given year might be trifling, but it was a symbol of his status in the firm. And, perhaps most important of all, it acknowledged his right to be informed of what was going on.

Joseph, who now had Seebohm's whole-hearted support, got his way. When Rowntrees' directors had considered William Wallace's report they decided to adopt the principle of profit-sharing, and a scheme was put into force in 1923. In the first fifteen years of its existence only two small distributions were made, but the scheme did not lose its popularity with the workers on that account. They knew the facts, and knew that a promise had been made to share the surplus profits as soon as there were any. In the ten years ending in 1953 one and a half million pounds were distributed among them.

In 1921, two years before Joseph retired, Rowntrees established their Appeal Committee. It was a logical development of the Firm's whole policy, but it was also a unique example of a court of justice being set up inside a factory. It brought into the world of industry, for the first time, the principle which is the foundation of English law—that everyone has the right to be tried by an impartial tribunal.

The Appeal Committee was composed of five people: two were elected by the workers, two were nominated by the directors, and the chairman had to be someone jointly appointed by the other four. Any employee who felt that some disciplinary action was unjust when taken against him for breach of a Works' Rule or for conduct not affecting the performance of his work, could appeal to this Committee. It had powers either to confirm the original decision, or to reduce or increase the penalties which the management had imposed. There was no right of appeal to the Committee in the case of an employee who was dismissed or had disciplinary action taken against him for conduct affecting the performance of his work; but anyone in this position, if he felt that injustice had been done, could appeal to the executive officer immediately above the one who had dismissed or penalized him. He could take his appeal, if necessary, all the way up the chain to the Chairman of the Board of Directors, whose decision was final. With such a procedure it was not easy for anyone to say, in the current phrase of the time, that 'he had been sacked because the foreman didn't like the colour of his eyes'.

In the first seventeen years of its existence the Appeal Committee heard thirty-one cases. Fifteen of them were concerned with theft, and ten of these appeals failed. But in four cases the penalties were reduced, and one worker was cleared entirely of the charge against him. Apart from the cases of theft, there were sixteen appeals against decisions made by the management. Seven of these decisions were upheld, in three cases penalties were reduced, and on six occasions the Committee gave a verdict in favour of the employee. Six persons' lives ran a different course because they had been able to challenge authority.

There cannot in 1921 have been many firms who were sitting easily enough in the saddle of power to give up their right to the last word in matters of discipline. These were years of bitter conflict, when one class of society could say that railwaymen were striking 'only for the right to get drunk', and another could sneer at 'capitalists with a conscience'; and when even many Quaker employers were frankly opposed to such things as Works Committees because they put too much power in the hands of the worker and lessened the management's authority.

There were plenty of people who told Joseph and Seebohm that the Appeal Committee was subversive of discipline; no possible good could come of it. But they were proved wrong. In spite of the fact that one of the decisions which the Committee reversed had been made by the Board of Directors themselves, their authority remained unimpaired.

'Authority depends upon justice,' Seebohm said, 'and it is always possible that a wrong judgement may be made. If it is, there should be machinery available to correct it.'

This was the purpose of the Appeal Committee, the body which seemed so strange and revolutionary to most contemporary employers. Yet, in essence, it was nothing new. Its roots went back to the grocer's shop in Pavement and the 'worrying watchful care' which had always guarded the individual interests of everyone who worked there from the time the elder Joseph had bought his business a hundred years before.

CHAPTER NINETEEN

IN 1923 Joseph retired from the position of Chairman of Rowntrees, and his son Seebohm took his place. It was seventy-one years since Joseph had started work as an apprentice for his father, and to go off to business every morning was second nature to him. He still went to the Cocoa Works on most days, walked about the familiar corridors, discussed new arrangements for the gardens which surrounded the factory, and sat in his room writing letters and articles. His mind was still alert; but now, occasionally, he let it wander towards the long past. He set down his impressions of the Irish potato famine, realizing perhaps how that distant summer journey had influenced his whole life. He began some 'recollections' of John Bright, remembering with affection the blunt-spoken, golden-voiced hero of his youth. Also, for a conference of the National Union of Railwaymen which was held in York in 1924, he wrote an article describing his travels by train nearly eighty years before. He had been taken by his governess to see the first train which ran to Scarborough from York, and he had stood on the walls of the city, in hot July sunshine, to watch it start its journey. He had travelled to Whitby, fourth-class, in a carriage without seats or roofing, and *that* train had been let down a steep incline on the moors by a rope. It was not, he observed, a satisfactory method; and quite soon a fatal accident led to the track being 'modified'.

Sitting at his desk in the room which had been his office ever since Tanner's Moat was abandoned, Joseph imprisoned these long-ago memories in handwriting which was still remarkably clear and steady. But he did not live in the past. People interested him as much as they had ever done, and his capacity for reading was undiminished.

During the winter of 1924–5 Joseph rented for some months Ramsay Macdonald's house in London. This house stood on

Downshire Hill, from which there is a view over half the city. One evening, standing at a window, Joseph looked down on the thousands of lights in row upon row of uninterrupted buildings. 'It's too big,' he said aloud. 'No one person can do anything for it.'

Perhaps he was remembering the smaller London he had loved in his early twenties; perhaps he was comparing it with his own business, whose size had become one of his major preoccupations. In either case the words acknowledged his awareness of a problem which was to trouble the future.

It was in London, in November 1924, that Joseph's wife died, five days after the fifty-seventh anniversary of their marriage. Many people had been afraid of Antoinette Rowntree in her time, and her relationship with the family into which she married had not been easy. But there were those who would always remember her with gratitude and respect. Most of her servants stayed with her for years, though she was an extremely exacting mistress. To the end of her life her household arrangements had a graceful orderliness about them which made an impression even upon casual young visitors. And some of these would also recall, with affection, her unexpectedly quick response to their most daring remarks.

Antoinette was never her husband's echo. She had her own tastes and her own opinions. Sometimes, no doubt, Joseph disagreed with her, but it seems unlikely that she ever bored him. She was a woman whose reactions were generally unpredictable, but in spite of all the difficulties of her temperament she enriched the family pattern in more ways than one. In her old age she still had the beautiful erect carriage of her girlhood, and her speech was as decisive as it had ever been. She left no uncertain mark on the minds of those who knew her.

For the last few months of his life Joseph lived alone at Clifton Lodge, and did not seem oppressed by his solitude. He was still able to enjoy the garden he had laid out, and he still went for his traditional 'Saturday Walk' by the sea at Scarborough. He had children and grandchildren living nearby, and he had not lost touch with the Cocoa Works. Although he no longer had any responsibility for the management of the Company he was a familiar figure to many of the people who worked there. His memory for faces remained very good, and he would sometimes turn and hurry back along a corridor if he fancied that he had passed without greeting some employee known to him.

One February morning Joseph was writing in his office at the Works when he complained of feeling cold. On the desk in front of him were some unfinished notes on John Bright. He was persuaded to leave them and go home to bed. The notes were never finished and he did not see the Cocoa Works again. He died five days later, in the early afternoon of February 24th.

The crowds who lined the streets on the day that Joseph was buried came to do honour to a great citizen of York. Among them were many who remembered his secret acts of kindness and his sound advice in private difficulties, as well as his public benefactions. Bricks and mortar told their own story. The ever-growing Cocoa Works, the tree-lined roads at New Earswick, the swimming-bath which he had built and given to the city, the public park and playing fields which had been the Company's war memorial to their staff who died in the First World War—all these stood as a plain statement of achievement, and the Trusts which he had founded would add further chapters to it in the future.

But the true record of Joseph's success lay elsewhere, not bounded by walls and windows, and not to be measured by trust funds. His legacy was not to York, but to the whole world of industry. Into that world, where there were few traditions and an 'unbridled scramble for the good things of life',[1] had been generally accepted as reasonable behaviour for a hundred years, he had brought other standards and different ideals. And calmly, unostentatiously, he had proved that they were sound—even in the sphere of big business.

He was no impractical idealist. Like every other business man he calculated his profits and counted his costs, but he never

[1] James Mill (1773–1836), father of John Stuart Mill.

thought of his business as something to be separated from the rest of his life. It was an inherited attitude. His father had seen nothing incongruous in mentioning his stocks of sugar and the Holy Spirit in the same paragraph of a letter, and it would never have occurred to Joseph that there might be a code of ethics applicable only to commerce.

He was deeply rooted in the Society of Friends, though he very rarely spoke in Meetings for Worship and seldom discussed his religious beliefs at any time. Perhaps he did not find it necessary since they were the air he breathed, the climate in which he was accustomed to live.

'Weave truth with trust' had once been blazoned by Courtauld's silk-weavers on a banner which they made for a present to their employers. It might have served for Joseph's motto. He had always trusted his workpeople and there had never been anything untrue in any of his dealings with them. Not once, but many times, he had taken a leap in the dark, putting his confidence in a policy which ran contrary to nearly all the beliefs of his day. The history of his Firm is punctuated with the phrase 'This was a new idea in industry'. He was an adventurer to the end of his life, for ever peering forward, never content with what had already been achieved.

There was very little chance, in his business, for grievances to grow up. His mind was usually a step ahead of his employees', and action was taken before anyone had thought of demanding it. His scholarship served him well, since it enabled him to see the wider implications behind the prosaic details of the day-to-day factory life. Quietly, with no dramatic gestures, the man who had been born in the reign of William IV made experiments which psychologists still find remarkable today.

Yet the basis of all his actions was the same. The change from paternalism to a democratic industrial policy, the welfare work, the pensions, the clubs, and committees—all the small steps forward which made up, in the end, an epic journey—had only one root. They were never simply a matter of expediency. They were the result of Joseph's true and unsentimental feeling for his workpeople, which was the core of the man himself.

There is an 'Essay on Capital' in Joseph's handwriting which seems to be the third in a series of lectures he gave—perhaps to the Adult School—on political economy. It is undated, but it expresses very clearly the motives which governed his whole long working life.

He speaks of the 'error of the older economists' in regarding the food and clothing of labourers as capital, and goes on to say, 'This error arises from regarding workmen as mere tools in the hand of the employer—tools that have to be supplied with food. It is a fault arising from a want of the historic sense, from thinking of the way in which industry happens to be conducted at present as if it were the only way in which it ever had been, or ever could be conducted. There is no reason why the employer should be looked upon as a different kind of being from his workmen. If he is necessary to the concern quite equally so are they. We shall reach a truer conclusion if we regard a business as a kind of partnership between masters and men, uniting their labour for a common end. This much more expresses the old way in which, long ago, industry *was* managed; and, though on a different scale, *it will increasingly have to be managed in the future.*'

The italics are Joseph's. He had heard the echoes from the past, and with them he challenged the future.

BOOKS CONSULTED

Everyday Things in England   Quenell
Quakers in Industry   Emden
Lord Shaftesbury and Social Industrial Progress   Bready
The Rise of Modern Industry   Hammond
The Town Labourer   Hammond
A Social History   Trevelyan
The Life of John Bright   Trevelyan
England Before and After Wesley   Bready
Methodism and the Working-class Movements of England
   Wearmouth
The British Working-class Movement   Cole
The Life of George Cadbury   Gardner
Early Victorian England 1830–65   Oxford University
   Press
The Life of Lord Carson   Marjoribanks
The Firm of Cadbury   Williams
British History in the Nineteenth Century   Trevelyan
Noble Lord, a Life of Lord Shaftesbury   Blackburn
A Memoir of Joseph Rowntree (1801–1859)   John Stephen-
   son Rowntree
Private Memoirs of Benjamin and Esther Seebohm
Journal of Elizabeth Rowntree (written between 1808 and 1835)
   In Manuscript
*Accounts of Yearly Meeting in 1855, 1857, and 1858, by
   Joseph Rowntree (1836–1925)*   In Manuscript
Journals of the Friends' Historical Society
John Stephenson Rowntree   Doncaster
The Seebohm Family of Bradford, York and Hitchin   Cud-
   worth
Quakerism and Industry. Reports of two Conferences of
   Employers in 1918 and 1928
Memoirs of Samuel Tuke
State Prohibition and Local Option   Joseph Rowntree and
   Arthur Sherwell
Public Control of the Liquor Traffic   Joseph Rowntree and
   Arthur Sherwell

Taxation of the Liquor Trade   Joseph Rowntree and Arthur Sherwell

The Temperance Problem and Social Reform   Joseph Rowntree and Arthur Sherwell

State Purchase of the Liquor Trade   Joseph Rowntree and Arthur Sherwell

British 'Gothenburg' Experiments   Joseph Rowntree and Arthur Sherwell

Public Interests and Trade Aggrandisement   Joseph Rowntree and Arthur Sherwell

Romance of a Great Industry   Mennell

Bootham School Magazine

The Human Factor in Business   Seebohm Rowntree

Poverty. A Study of Town Life   Seebohm Rowntree

Reports of Lecture Conferences, 1919–32, for Works Directors, Managers, Foremen and Forewomen, arranged by Seebohm Rowntree

'The York Bond of Brothers.' Letters from apprentices of Joseph Rowntree, Senior   In Manuscript

The *Cocoa Works Magazine*

Betting Newspapers and Quakerism   Pamphlet

A Reply to the Above   Pamphlet

Quaker Dress, 1640–1840   Saxon Snell

John Ford—a Quaker Schoolmaster   Stroud

Tom Brown's Schooldays   Hughes

Friends Face Reality   Loukes

Sybil: or The Two Nations   Disraeli

John Bright and the Quakers   Mills-Travis

New Times, New Methods, and New Men   Clarke

A Hundred Years of Economic Development in Great Britain   Jones and Poole

Last Essays   Young

Victorian England, Portrait of an Age   Young

Victorian People   Briggs

Ideas and Beliefs of the Victorians   Annan

The Making of Scientific Management   Urwick and Brech

Dynamic Administration   Follett

Problems of Growth in Industrial Undertakings   Urwick

A Time for Greatness   Agar

Roaring Century   Cruikshank

Strange Death of Liberal England   Dangerfield

England in the 1880s   Lynd

Rule of Democracy   Halevy

History of Liquor Licencing in England   Webb

Alcohol: Social and Economic Aspects   A collection of
   essays published by Gollancz
Alcohol and the Nation   Wilson
English Temperance Movement   Carter
Control of the Drink Trade   Carter
One Man's Vision   Waddilove
Arnold Rowntree   Vipont
Uncommon People   Bloomfield
The Acquisitive Society   Tawney
Self-Help   Smiles
Thrift   Smiles
Portrait of England between the Exhibitions, 1851–1951
   Lindsay and Washington
Are Workers Human?   Taylor
Joint Consultation in British Industry   National Institute
   of Industrial Psychology
Big Business   Drucker
Clifton Lodge   Thompson

INDEX

A

Ackworth School, 23
Adult School, 50–1, 56, 60, 74, 80, 116, 130, 154, 156, 198
Advertising, 80–1, 90, 121, 124, 166
Alcoholics Anonymous, 141
Annual Address to Shareholders, 186 Employees, 186
Answers, 160
Appeal Committee, 191–3
Apprentices, 13, 14, 22, 23, 25, 31–6, 37, 49, 55, 57, 118, 124
Archer, 90, 92
Arkwright, 147
Arnold, Dr, 28
Asquith, 160

B

Backhouse, Hannah, 21 James, 12, 13
Bad Pyrmont Meeting, 44
Bedford, Peter, 44
Beveridge Report, 179
Blossom Street, 25, 30, 158
Bonus systems, 113
'Bookeries', 124
Booth, Charles, 130, 144
Bootham, No. 19, 77, 87
Bootham School, 23, 25, 27, 28, 30, 45, 55, 56, 77, 87
Bootham School Natural History Society, 28
Bournville (factory), 40 (village), 147
Bright, Jacob, 52 John, 11, 17, 30, 37, 39, 43, 47, 51, 52, 78, 79, 104, 152, 194, 196

Bristol Conference of Adult School Teachers, 62
British 'Gothenburg' Experiments, 139
British Museum, 66
British School, Hope Street, 50, 130
Burtt, Joseph, 176

C

Cadbury Brothers, 147, 164, 173, 176 George, 40, 84, 154, 173, 175
Castlegate School (later The Mount), 44, 45
Chartists, 11
Cholera, 60
Church and State, 63, 64, 155
Church Schools, 182
Classes at Cocoa Works, 124
Clifton Lodge, 158, 159
Clubs at Cocoa Works (Cricket, Angling, Camera, Bowling, Cycling, Football, Tennis), 124 197
Cobbett, 11
Cobden, 30, 42, 43
Cocoa manufacturing processes, 72. 84, 90, 108
'Cocoa Press', 173
'Cocoa Scandal', 176
Cocoa Works Debating Society, 98
Cocoa Works Magazine, 127–8, 129. 163, 165, 182, 185
'Company System', 134, 136
'Congo Horrors', 174
Conservative Party, 159, 160, 173
Continuation Classes, 165

Corn Laws, 11, 30, 37, 42
Courtauld, firm of, 95, 96, 197
    Samuel, 96
Crichton, David, 127
Cross, Richard, 162
Crossley John, & Sons, 171
    Martha, 171

D

Daily Chronicle, 134
Daily Mail, 160
Daily Mirror, 160
Daily News, 134, 173
Disraeli, Benjamin, 41, 163
Domestic School at Cocoa Works,
    165
Drink, 131, 132, 133

E

Echo, 175
Education Act, 78, 184
Edward VII, 160, 163
Egyptian Campaign, 104
'Elect' cocoa, 90–1, 121, 124
Established Church, 15, 63, 65, 79,
    177
Exhibition Buildings, 124

F

Factory Departmental Councils, 186
Fines, 112–13
Follett, Mary, 186
Ford, John, 27–9
Foremen and forewomen, 112–13
    appointment of, 188–9
Fox, George, 15, 79, 177
Frankland, Henry, 71
Free Library, 178
Free Trade, 104
Freedom of the City, 177
Friedensthal, 66
Friendly Societies, 75

Fruit Room, 115
Fry, Sir Edward, 174, 175
    Elizabeth, 17, 20
    J. Storrs, 62, 63

G

Gaget, Claude, 84, 89
Gambling, 173–5
George V, 160
George, Lloyd, 159, 164
Gillet, George, 67
Gladstone, William Ewart, 40, 42,
    78, 104, 119, 163
'Gothenburg' experiment, 135, 136,
    139
Government monopoly of spirits,
    134
Gums and pastilles, 84, 85, 86, 89,
    115
Gurney, Samuel, 39

H

Hanks, 74, 82
Hardy, Thomas, 180
Haxby Road, 102, 107, 109, 115, 124,
    126
Hipsley, Henry, 71
Hitchin, 66, 67
Holidays with pay, 188
Hollander, Cornelius, 90
Hotham, Elizabeth, 55
House of Commons, 39, 41–3, 127,
    173
House of Lords, 104, 159, 160
Hustler, Sarah, 44, 45

I

Industrial Policy, 110–11, 197
    Revolution, 10, 60, 93, 118, 125,
        133, 138
    Welfare, 96, 97, 98, 109–10, 125,
        129

Ireland, 37, 60, 181
   Famine, 29, 179, 194
   Home Rule, 104

J

Jamaica, 63
Journeys abroad, 57, 59, 83, 84, 85,
   86, 101, 120

L

Law, Bonar, 173
Layard, Sir Austin Henry, 43
Leeman, George, 78
Lever, Sir George, 147
Liberal Association, 130, 156
*Life and Labour of the People of
   London*, 130, 144
Lister, Joseph, 39
Livesey, Joseph, 132, 139–41
Local Option, 140–1

M

Macdonald, Dr Peter, 164
Macdonald, Ramsay, 194
Manchester Guardian, 175
Massingham, H. W., 162
Merchant Adventurers' Company,
   70, 142
More, Hannah, 12
Morning Leader, 173
Morrel, J. Bowes, 120, 162
Mount School, 45, 55, 56, 58, 105
Municipal elections, 178

N

Nation, 163
National Insurance Act, 164
National Union of Railwaymen, 194
Negro slavery, 63
Nevinson, W. H., 176
New Earswick, 147–50, 153, 156,
   177, 185, 196

Folk Hall, 182
Football Club, 182
School, 183–4
Village Council, 182
New Statesman, 162
Northern Echo, 161, 162

O

Oldknow, 147
One Man's Vision, 147, 150
Opium traffic, 174
Opium war, 63
*Opportunities and Dangers of
   Wealth*, 152
Owen, Robert, 147

P

Palmerston, 43
Park, 196
Parker, Hon. Reginald, 158
Pauperism in England and Wales,
   62
Pavement house and shop, 10, 12,
   13, 14, 16, 18–20, 22–4, 29, 31,
   36, 40, 43, 46, 49, 54–5, 57, 59,
   68, 76, 88, 93, 104, 107, 116,
   131, 143, 152, 153, 158, 193
Peace Testimony, 184
Pensions, 114–15, 166–70, 197
People's Budget, 159
People's Palaces, 138, 141
People's Refreshment House
   Association, 135
Piecework, 113
'Plain dress', 47, 53–4, 106
Poor Laws, 61
Port Sunlight, 147
Portuguese Government, 176
Poverty, 29–30, 60–4, 130, 178–9
Poverty, a Study of Town Life, 143,
   144, 146
Profit sharing, 110, 170, 171, 187,
   189–91
Prohibition, 134–5

Public Control of the Liquor Traffic, 139

Public House Trust Companies, 135

Public Interest or Trade Aggrandisement, 139

Public Library, 130

Purey-Cust, Dean, 177

Q

Quaker Marriage Regulations, 16, 36–7, 47–8, 51–2, 55

Schools, 130, 154

R

Reckitt, Sir James, 147

Reform Bill, 104

Retreat, The, 71, 130

Rothschild, Baron, 43

Rowntree & Co., 120

Agnes, 76, 88

Arnold, 111, 120, 121, 124, 162, 184

Elizabeth, 13

Emma Antoinette (Seebohm), 66, 68, 77, 87, 145, 195

Frank, 111, 120

Hannah, 24, 57, 59, 67, 85

Henry Isaac, 14, 30, 67, 68, 71, 72, 73, 75, 76, 81, 82, 84, 85, 86, 88, 92, 102, 104, 108, 111, 121, 151, 167

John (the elder), 13

John Stephenson, 14, 22, 23, 26, 28, 29, 30, 31, 46, 47, 50, 51, 54, 55, 56, 64, 67, 85, 98, 111, 116

John Wilhelm, 68, 76, 77, 79, 83, 86, 87, 88, 89, 90, 92, 101, 105, 106, 111, 120, 122, 123, 144, 151, 154, 180, 185

Joseph (senior), 12, 13, 14, 16, 18, 19, 21, 22, 23, 24, 25, 29, 31, 34, 35, 36, 37, 38, 40, 43, 46, 47, 51, 52, 54, 55, 71, 72, 81, 143, 158, 193

Joseph, Birth, 10

Childhood, 18–24

Schooldays, 27–8

Apprenticeship, 31–5

First marriage, 56

Second marriage, 67

Partnership with Henry Isaac, 69

Freedom of City, 177–9

Retirement, 194

Death, 169

Joshua, 59, 65, 162

Julia (Seebohm), 44, 45, 46, 56, 58, 59, 61, 64, 67, 69, 104

'Lilley', 58, 59, 67, 68, 69

Oscar, 80, 87

Sarah Jane, 24, 26

Sarah Stephenson, 11, 14, 18, 20, 22, 23, 24, 45, 55, 57, 67, 87, 104

Seebohm, 76, 77, 88, 90, 106, 107, 111, 113, 114, 115, 120, 122, 123, 143, 144, 146, 147, 166, 185, 188, 189, 190, 192, 193, 194

'Stephen', 80, 106, 107

Theodore, 120

Winifred, 87

Royal Commission on Depression of Trade, (1886), 86

Housing, 137

Licensing, 141

S

St Mary's, 37, 56, 87, 105

Salisbury, Lord, 162

Satterthwaite, Thomas, 53

'Saturday walks', 116–17, 125, 195

Seebohm, Benjamin, 44, 45, 58, 66, 83

Esther Wheeler, 45, 56, 58, 64, 65

Frederic, 65–6

Henry, 65–6

Wilhelm, 66

Selborne, Lord, 160

Shaftesbury, Lord, 12, 30
Sherwell, Arthur, 131, 133, 134, 136, 139, 142
Shop Stewards, 186
Sibford School, 43
Smiles, Samuel, 171, 190
Smollett, Tobias George, 133
Society of Friends, 14–17, 19, 20, 27–9, 33, 36, 38–9, 45, 48, 51–4, 55, 56, 64–5, 77, 106, 124, 131, 151, 153, 154, 156, 174, 197
Soup Kitchen, 29, 61, 154
Star, 173, 175
Statistics on poverty, 60–1, 74, 114
Strikes, 181, 187
Sturge, Samuel, 53
Suggestions Scheme, 129
Sweated industries, 174
Swimming-bath, 196

T

Tanner's Moat, 68, 73–80, 83–6, 88, 90–3, 97–9, 102, 107, 108–9, 111, 112, 114, 115, 126, 128, 129, 151, 167–8, 170
Tasker, Mary, 19, 20
Taxation of the Liquor Trade, The, 139
Temperance Movement, 139, 140, 141
Temperance Problem and Social Reform, The, 131, 134, 140, 143
Thistlethwaite, William, 53
Times, 134
Titbits, 90, 160
'Top House', 37, 56–7, 104–6, 119, 144, 158
Trade Unions, 75, 172, 186, 190
Truck Act, 113
Trusts, 64, 148, 153–6, 160–2, 173, 175, 182–4, 196

Tuke & Co., 71–3
Mary, 70–1
Samuel, 71
William, 44–5, 71

U

United Kingdom Alliance, 140, 141
Universities, 15
Unwin, Raymond, 149

W

Waddilove, L. E., 147, 150
Wallace, William, 190, 191
'Waste', 112–13
Webb, Beatrice and Sidney, 172
Wedgwood, firm of, 95
Welfare, 187, 197
Welfare State, 144
Wellington, Duke of, 133
Westminster Press, 161
Westow, 145
Whateley, 65
Whitley Committee, 186
Widows' Benefit Fund, 169
Wilberforce, William, 12
William IV, 197
Woodbrooke Settlement, 154
Working hours, 82, 99, 188
Works' Committees, 192
Councils, 186, 187
Dentist, 164
Doctor, 164
Library, 94
Rules, 187, 192
World, 173

Y

Yearly Meeting, 1855, 38–9
1857, 46–8
1858, 51–3, 54
'York Bond of Brothers', 34–5

OTHER QUAKER BOOKS
available from Quaker Bookshops or direct from Sessions of York, England

THE BEGINNINGS OF QUAKERISM (to about 1660) — The Standard work by Wm. C. Braithwaite. Reprinted 1981.

THE SECOND PERIOD OF QUAKERISM (to about 1725) also by Wm. C. Braithwaite. Reprinted 1979.

BARCLAY'S APOLOGY in modern English — edited by Dean Freiday. Reprint 1980. This statement of Quaker principles was first issued in Latin in 1676 and in English in 1678.

NO CROSS, NO CROWN by William Penn. Reprint of the 1682 edition, together with 1930 introduction and 1981 foreword.

QUAKER ENCOUNTERS by John Ormerod Greenwood in three volumes
    Volume I   Friends and Relief (published 1975)
    Volume II   Vines on the Mountains (published 1977)
    Volume III Whispers of Truth (published 1978)
  A history series on Quaker relief, missionary and overseas service.

THE FRIENDS MEETING HOUSE by Hubert Lidbetter, FRIBA. Historical Survey of Friends' places of Worship from the beginning of Quakerism including plans and photographs. Reprinted 1979.

LAUGHTER IN QUAKER GREY and MORE QUAKER LAUGHTER
  Two volumes by William H. Sessions of humorous Quaker anecdotes.

FRIENDS IN YORK by Stephen Allott. The Quaker Story from 1651 in the life of a Meeting.

THE TUKES OF YORK. Presented by W. K. & E. M. Sessions. Narrative of the well-known York Quaker Family.

SOMERSET ANTHOLOGY by Roger Clark. 24 pieces written for the Village Essay Society of Street, Somerset — edited by Percy A. Lovell.

A HISTORY OF SHOE MAKING IN STREET, SOMERSET: C. and J. Clark, 1833-1903, by G. B. Sutton.

LUKE HOWARD 1772-1864. His correspondence with Goethe and his continental journey of 1816. Edited with commentary by Emeritus Professor D. F. S. Scott.

ENERGY UNBOUND by Kenneth C. Barnes. The history of Wennington School.

CAROLINE FOX 1819-1871: Quaker Blue stocking of Plymouth: Friend of John Stuart Mill and Thomas Carlyle, by Robert Tod.

WILLIAM FRYER HARVEY 1885-1937, A Friend with a Difference, by Rev. C. E. J. Fryer

WOODBROOKE 1953-1978. The 3rd 25 years by F. Ralph Barlow, edited by David B. Gray.